A Book of Advent and Christmas Prayers

Other Loyola Press books
by William G. Storey

**The Complete Rosary
A Guide to Praying the Mysteries**

**A Prayer Book of Catholic Devotions
Praying the Seasons and Feasts of the Church Year**

**Novenas
Prayers of Intercession and Devotion**

A Catholic Book of Hours and Other Devotions

Prayers of Christian Consolation

**A Beginner's Book of Prayer
An Introduction to Traditional Catholic Prayers**

A Prayer Book for Eucharistic Adoration

**A Book of Marian Prayers
A Compilation of Marian Devotions from
the Second to the Twenty-First Century**

A Book of Lenten Prayers

A Book of Advent and Christmas Prayers

Composed, edited, and translated by
William G. Storey
Professor Emeritus of Liturgy
University of Notre Dame

LOYOLA PRESS.
A JESUIT MINISTRY

Chicago

LOYOLA PRESS.
A JESUIT MINISTRY

3441 N. Ashland Avenue
Chicago, Illinois 60657
(800) 621-1008
www.loyolapress.com

© 2013 William G. Storey
All rights reserved

In accordance with c. 827, permission to publish is granted on April 15, 2013, by Rev. Msgr. John F. Canary, Vicar General of the Archdiocese of Chicago. Permission to publish is an official declaration of ecclesiastical authority that the material is free from doctrinal and moral error. No legal responsibility is assumed by the grant of this permission.

Copyright acknowledgments appear on pages 230–232 and constitute a continuation of this copyright page.

Cover and interior design by Donna Antkowiak

ISBN-13: 978-0-8294-3901-4

ISBN-10: 0-8294-3901-3

Library of Congress Control Number: 2013937781

Printed in China
13 14 15 16 17 RRD/China 10 9 8 7 6 5 4 3 2 1

Contents

Introduction ix

Part 1: The Season of Advent 1
A Devotion for the Season of Advent 1
An Advent Litany for Each Day 16
Advent Prayers at Meals 17
A Novena for Advent 19

Part 2: Devotions for Feasts During Advent 23
The Immaculate Conception of Mary 23
The Nativity of the Virgin Mary 31
Mary's Presentation in the Temple 38
Saint Nicholas of Myra in Lycia 44
Our Lady of Guadalupe 50
The Espousals of Mary and Joseph 58
The Annunciation of the Lord 64

Saint Joseph of Nazareth............................74
The Visitation of Mary to Elizabeth......81
Saint John the Baptist 89

Part 3: Devotions for the Feasts of Christmastide 99

Christmas Eve 99
Christmas Week 104
The Feast of the Holy Family...........115
Comites Christi: The Companions of Christ...................................121
Saint Stephen, the First Martyr 122
Saint John the Evangelist 128
The Holy Innocents of Bethlehem.......135
Saint Thomas of Canterbury............140
The Infant Jesus 146
Solemnity of the Mother of God 154
The Vigil of the Epiphany................162
The Epiphany.............................168
The Presentation of Jesus in the Temple. 178
Christ's Return Out of Egypt 186
Jesus at Twelve Years of Age............194

Part 4: Prayers for Christmas and Advent ... 199

The Daily Angelus ... 199

To Our Lady Mother ... 201

The Coming ... 202

Mary and Eve ... 203

Saint Francis of Assisi and Christmas at Greccio ... 204

A Prayer to the Child Jesus ... 206

Before the Paling of the Stars ... 207

To St. John the Baptist ... 208

The Nativity of Christ ... 208

The One Mediator ... 209

In Excelsis Gloria ... 210

A Christmas Devotion ... 210

Carol ... 215

The Virgin Mary ... 216

Tota pulchra es, Maria ... 216

Antiphon for the Virgin ... 217

Christmas Eve Prayers ... 218

The Flight into Egypt 219

Notes 221

Acknowledgments 230

About the Author 233

Introduction

Christmas the Season

Apart from the New Passover (Easter), the church calendar grew very slowly during the first two centuries. In the fourth century, two new celebrations emerged in what was becoming the beginning of the church year: the Nativity of Jesus (Christmas) on December 25 and the Epiphany on January 6. Christmas grew up in the churches of the Latin West while the Epiphany came into being in the churches of the East. The theme of Christmas was the birth of Jesus, while the theme of the East was his baptism. By the late fourth century, Christmas was adopted in the East, while the Epiphany was appropriated in the West with its major theme the coming of the Magi.

Advent as a preparation for Christmas emerged a bit later than these primeval feasts. Originally Advent was considered a penitential time of prayer and fasting, but that meaning faded away as newer feasts surfaced in Advent and in the week of Christmas.

This prayer book encompasses the entire story of Jesus's coming, from the immaculate conception of his mother Mary to his life at twelve years of age. The first part offers devotions for the season of Advent. Part two provides devotions for the great feasts during Advent. This is the first part of the narrative of Jesus's coming—the immaculate conception through the consecration of John the Baptist. The story continues in the third part of the book—Devotions for the Feasts of Christmastide. These include the great feasts of Christmas and Epiphany. The fourth and last part of the book is a collection of shorter prayers for Advent and Christmastide.

POINTERS FOR PRAYER

For Christians of the Catholic tradition, prayer is daily, weekly, and seasonal. *Daily* prayer is morning and evening prayer to start and finish our day. *Weekly* is for Mass every Sunday and special holy days, and for many Catholics, weekday Mass when possible.

This is a book of *seasonal* prayer for Advent and the Christmas season. This prayer immerses us in the coming of Christ as a baby in the manger of Bethlehem and in the rest of his childhood. These strong seasons ask us to concentrate on the religious meaning of these events so that we can absorb and appropriate them in our hearts and in our behavior.

The devotions in this prayer book are composed of psalms and canticles from the Old and New Testament, readings from Scripture and the holy Fathers, and readings from other Catholic writers and poets. Other material includes hymns from the long musical history of the Church and an extensive collection of litanies and prayers from the Roman Missal and other sources of prayer.

These prayers are meant to be prayed *carefully*, observing the punctuation; *slowly*, by pronouncing each syllable and word as if they were freshly coined; and *clearly*, by saying them as reverently as being repeated in the very ear of God. These are the great prayers of our Catholic tradition. When we pray them with faith, hope, and love, we will be on the path to holiness. Praying with steadiness, patience, and persistence, following in Jesus, the way, the truth, and the life, we shall come to know him as he really is.

How to Pray

People who pray alone—and they will be many—may adopt the postures that suit them best. The important thing to remember is that we pray in the presence of the Blessed Trinity and the whole court of heaven.

People who pray in groups may try postures that facilitate common prayer: standing for hymns, psalms, and canticles; sitting for readings and reflection; kneeling for litanies and the final prayers.

Groups should have a leader, and another person should be chosen for the readings.

A Place to Pray

Some of us can drop in to pray at an open church or chapel, but most of us will only be able to pray at home. Even there, it is still a challenge to find a quiet place or time for our daily prayers. A prayer corner helps. This might be a special place for family prayer with holy pictures, a Bible, candles, flowers, and even incense. If that is too hard to create or find, try for a remote bedroom, an attic, or a basement corner for private prayer. It will be worth it.

Being adaptable is very important for both private and group use of these devotions. This is especially true with young children; just one or two elements of a devotion would be advisable for them. But even older children and adults need to consider how much and how they should pray each time. Common sense is required in prayer as in the rest of life. If time is short or one is very tired or ill, pray just a little. If we are in good health and spirits, we should try to pray the whole devotion in one sitting—carefully, slowly, and reverently.

The Athanasian Creed

The Athanasian Creed is a very old and venerable Latin creed, probably composed in Southern Gaul in the late fifth or early sixth century by an anonymous author. This section of it is a profession of faith in the incarnation of Our Lord that reflects the orthodox teaching of both the Council of Ephesus (431) and the Council of Chalcedon (451) and was used in the Medieval and Tridentine Breviaries where it was required on most Sundays at the office of Prime. It is provided here as a dogmatic background for all the devotional contents of this prayer book.

It is necessary to eternal salvation that we believe faithfully in
 the Incarnation of our Lord Jesus Christ.
The right faith therefore is, that we believe and confess
 that our Lord Jesus Christ, the Son of God, is God and Man;
God, of the substance of the Father, begotten before the worlds:
 and Man, of the substance of his Mother, born in the world;
Perfect God, perfect Man, of a reasoning soul and human flesh subsisting;
Equal to the Father as touching his Godhead;
 and inferior to the Father as touching his Manhood.

Who, although he be God and Man, yet he be not two,
  but one Christ;
One, however, not by conversion of the Godhead
  into flesh, but by taking of the Manhood into God;
One altogether, not by confusion of Substance,
  but by unity of Person.
For as the reasoning soul and flesh is one man,
  so God and Man is one Christ;
Who suffered for our salvation, descended into hell,
  rose again the third day from the dead.
He ascended into heaven, he sits at the right hand
  of the Father, Almighty God, from which he shall
  come to judge the living and the dead.
At whose coming all shall rise again with their bodies
  and shall give account for their own works.
And they that have done good shall go into eternal life;
  and they that have done evil into eternal fire.
This is the Catholic faith, which except we believe faithfully,
  we cannot be safe/saved.[1]

I
The Season of Advent

A Devotion for the Season of Advent

The season of Advent is roughly four weeks long; it begins on the Sunday on or nearest the feast of St. Andrew the Apostle (November 30) and lasts until Christmas Eve. Advent is a season of comings, arrivals, and encounters.

John the Baptist appears as the herald of the coming Messiah, preaching repentance, conversion, and baptism in the river Jordan (Mark 1:1–11). The archangel Gabriel comes as a messenger of the Most High to Mary of Nazareth and asks her to accept in faith the mission and destiny of being the mother of the Messiah (Luke 1:26–38). An angel of the Lord appears to Joseph, Mary's betrothed, in a dream, and tells him not to be afraid to take an already pregnant Mary as his bride (Matthew 1:18–23).

In this season marked by such scriptural anticipation, we await in expectant awe for the birth of Jesus, for his manifestation to the shepherds and the Magi, for his revelation to the two ancients, Simeon and Anna, for his loss and finding again in the temple, and finally, for his baptism by John in the Jordan and the beginning of the messianic era of preaching and healing.

Underlying all these divine events is another and even more awesome coming, the ultimate revealing of the Son of God, "who will come again in glory to judge the living and the dead" (Nicean Creed).

The liturgy is not just a mental commemoration of past events; these saving events are present in the sacraments of the worshipping church. "What we could see in our Redeemer while he was on earth has now passed over into sacraments." (St. Leo the Great)[2]

> God took on human nature that we might take on divine nature.
> **St. Augustine of Hippo Regius (354–430)**[3]

This devotion for the whole of Advent contains many options: choices of Psalms, four choices of readings for each of the four weeks, and four sets of closing prayers. Choose the options that suit the appropriate week.

Leader: Your light ✝ will come, O Jerusalem.

All: ~The Lord will dawn on you in radiant beauty.

Leader: The sign of the cross shall appear in the heavens,

All: ~When our Lord comes to judge the world.

Psalm 117 RGP   **A Call to Praise and Prayer**

The leader begins the antiphon to the asterisk * and the group finishes the rest of the antiphon.

Antiphon Come, let us sing to the Lord, *
   who comes as our Redeemer.

O praise the Lord, all you nations;
acclaim him, all you peoples!
For his merciful love has prevailed over us;
and the Lord's faithfulness endures forever.

Antiphon Come, let us sing to the Lord,
   who comes as our Redeemer.

Glory to the Father, and to the Son,
   and to the Holy Spirit:
as it was in the beginning, is now,
   and will be for ever. Amen.

Antiphon Come, let us sing to the Lord,
   who comes as our Redeemer.

The stanzas of the hymn are varied between the leader and the group.

Hymn

Come, O long-expected Jesus,
Born to set your people free;
From our fears and sins release us;
Free us from captivity.

Israel's strength and consolation,
You the hope of all the earth,
Dear desire of every nation,
Joy of every longing heart.

Born your people to deliver,
Born a child and yet a king!

Born to reign in us for ever,
Now your gracious kingdom bring.

By your own eternal Spirit
Rule in all our hearts alone;
By your all-sufficient merit
Raise us to your glorious throne.

Charles Wesley (1707–1788)[4]

We pray one or more of the following three items.

1. Psalm 85 RGP
The Age of Justice and Peace

The leader begins the antiphon to the asterisk * and the group finishes the rest of the antiphon.

Antiphon God will speak peace * TO THE PEOPLE.

O LORD, you have favored your land,
and brought back the captives of Jacob.
You forgave the guilt of your people,
and covered all their sins.
You averted all your rage;
you turned back the heat of your anger.

Bring us back, O God, our savior!
Put an end to your grievance against us.
Will you be angry with us forever?
Will your anger last from age to age?

Will you not restore again our life,
that your people may rejoice in you?
Let us see, O LORD, your mercy,
and grant us your salvation.

I will hear what the Lord God speaks;
he speaks of peace for his people and his faithful,
and those who turn their hearts to him.
His salvation is near for those who fear him,
and his glory will dwell in our land.

Merciful love and faithfulness have met;
justice and peace have kissed.
Faithfulness shall spring from the earth,
and justice look down from the heaven.

Also the Lord will bestow his bounty,
and our earth shall yield its increase.
Justice will march before him,
and guide his steps on the way.

All recite the whole antiphon.

Antiphon God will speak peace to the people.

Psalm Prayer

Leader:

Let us pray (pause for silent prayer):

God of our salvation,
in the time of Jesus, your anointed Son,
justice and peace shall kiss each other
as you bring to completion all the promises
made to your holy prophets.
Pardon all our sins,
and speak peace to the people,
who turn to God in their hearts.
Blest be Jesus, now and for ever.
All: ~Amen.

2. A Canticle of Isaiah the Prophet 11:1–9 NAB

*The leader begins the antiphon to the asterisk * and the group finishes the rest of the antiphon.*

Antiphon On that day the root of Jesse * shall stand as a signal to the peoples.

A shoot shall sprout from the stump of Jesse,
 and from his roots a bud shall blossom.
The spirit of the Lord shall rest upon him,
 a spirit of wisdom and understanding,
a spirit of counsel and of strength,
 a spirit of knowledge and of fear of the Lord,
and his delight shall be the fear of the Lord.

Not by appearance shall he judge,
 nor by hearsay shall he decide,
but he shall judge the poor with justice,
 and shall decide aright for the land's afflicted.

He shall strike the ruthless with the rod of
  his mouth,
 and with the breath of his lips he shall slay the
  wicked.
Justice shall be the band around his waist,
 and faithfulness a belt upon his hips.

Then the wolf shall be a guest of the lamb,
 and the leopard shall lie down with the kid;
the calf and the young lion shall browse together,
 with a little child to guide them.

The cow and the bear shall be neighbors,
  together their young shall rest;
  the lion shall eat hay like the ox.
The baby shall play by the cobra's den
  and the child lay his hand on the adder's lair.

There shall be no harm or ruin on all my holy mountain;
  for the earth shall be filled with the knowledge of the Lord,
  as waters cover the sea.

All recite the whole antiphon.

Antiphon On that day the root of Jesse shall stand as a signal to the peoples.

Psalm Prayer

Let us pray (pause for silent prayer):

May Jesus, the Messiah and Lord,
the descendant of Jesse and David,
pour out his Spirit on humankind
for the welfare of all nations and peoples
that stand in awe of him;
for his reign is a reign for all ages.
All: ~Amen.

3. A Canticle of Isaiah the Prophet

40:3–5, 9 NAB

The leader begins the antiphon to the asterisk * and the group finishes the rest of the antiphon.

Antiphon You, child, shall be called the prophet of the Most High; * for you will go before the Lord to prepare the way.

A voice cries out:
"In the wilderness prepare the way
   of the Lord,
make straight in the desert a highway
   for our God.

Every valley shall be lifted up,
and every mountain and hill be made low;
the uneven ground shall become level,
and the rough places plain.

Then the glory of the Lord shall be revealed,
and all people shall see it together,
for the mouth of the Lord has spoken."

Get you up to a high mountain, O Zion,
   herald of good tidings;
lift up your voice with strength,
O Jerusalem, herald of good tidings,
lift it up, do not fear;
say to the cities of Judah,
"Here is your God!"

All recite the whole antiphon.

Antiphon You, child, shall be called the prophet of the Most High; for you will go before the Lord to prepare the way.

Psalm Prayer

Let us pray (pause for silent prayer):

At your Son's first coming among us,
O Most High God,
you commissioned John the Baptist
as the forerunner of the Lord Messiah.
By his example and prayers,
prepare us to celebrate worthily
the mysteries of the Word made flesh,
full of grace and truth.
Blest be the name of Jesus, now and for ever.
All: ~Amen.

Readings for the Four Weeks of Advent:

The reader recites the whole reading and leads the responsory.

1. God's House   Isaiah 2:1–3

In the days to come
  the mountain of the Lord's house
shall be established as the highest of the mountains,
  and shall be raised above all the hills;
all the nations shall stream to it.
  Many peoples shall come and say,
"Come, let us go up to the mountain of the Lord,
  to the house of the God of Jacob;
that he may teach us his ways
  and that we may walk in his paths."

Quiet prayer

Responsory

Reader: Drop down dew you heavens from above,
All: ~Drop down dew you heavens from above,

And let the earth bud forth a Savior, alleluia!
~Drop down dew you heavens from above,

Glory to the Father, and to the Son,
 and to the Holy Spirit:
~Drop down dew you heavens from above.

2. The Salvation of Our God   Isaiah 52:7–8,10

How beautiful upon the mountains are the feet of the messenger who announces peace, who brings good news, who announces salvation, who says to Zion, "Your God reigns." Listen, your sentinels lift up their voices, together they sing for joy; for in plain sight they see the return of the Lord to Zion. The Lord has bared his holy arm before the eyes of all the nations; and all the ends of the earth shall see the salvation of our God.

Pause for quiet prayer.

Responsory

Let your face shine on us, O Lord of hosts,
~Let your face shine on us, O Lord of hosts,

And we shall be saved.
~Let your face shine on us, O Lord of hosts,

Glory to the Father, and to the Son,
  and to the Holy Spirit:
~Let your face shine on us, O Lord of hosts.

3. Rejoice in the Lord!   Philippians 4:4–7

Brothers and sisters, Rejoice in the Lord always; again I will say, Rejoice. Let your gentleness be known to everyone. The Lord is near. Do not worry about anything, but in everything by prayer and supplication with thanksgiving let your requests be made known to God. And the peace of God, which surpasses all understanding, will guard your hearts and your minds in Christ Jesus.

Pause for quiet prayer.

Responsory

Look, the Virgin is with child,
~Look, the Virgin is with child,

And she shall bear a Son.
~Look, the Virgin is with child,

Glory to the Father, and to the Son,
  and to the Holy Spirit:
~Look, the Virgin is with child.

4. Excellence   Philippians 4:8–9

Finally, beloved, whatever is true, whatever is honorable, whatever is just, whatever is pure, whatever is pleasing, whatever is commendable, if there is any excellence and if there is anything worthy of praise, think about these things. Keep on doing the things that you have learned and received and heard and seen in me, and the God of peace will be with you.

Pause for quiet prayer.

Responsory

Hail, Mary, full of grace, alleluia!
~Hail, Mary, full of grace, alleluia!

The Lord is with you, alleluia!
~Hail, Mary, full of grace, alleluia!

Glory to the Father, and to the Son,
 and to the Holy Spirit:
~Hail, Mary, full of grace, alleluia!

The Canticle of Zachary   Luke 1:68–79 ELLC

This canticle is to be recited each day.

The leader begins the antiphon to the asterisk * and the group finishes the rest of the antiphon.

Antiphon Like the sun in the morning,*
 the Savior of the world will dawn.
 Like rain on the meadows he will descend.

Blessed are you, † Lord, the God of Israel,
you have come to their people and set them free.
You have raised up for us a mighty Savior,
born of the house of your servant David.
Through your holy prophets, you promised of old
 to save us from our enemies,
 from the hands of all who hate us,

to show mercy to our forebears,
and to remember your holy covenant.
This was the oath you swore to our father
 Abraham:
to set us free from the hands of our enemies,
free to worship you without fear,
holy and righteous before you,
all the days of our life.

And you, child, shall be called the prophet of the
 Most High,
for you will go before the Lord to prepare the way,
to give God's people knowledge of salvation
by the forgiveness of their sins.
In the tender compassion of our God
the dawn from on high shall break upon us,
to shine on those who dwell in darkness
 and the shadow of death,
and to guide our feet into the way of peace.

To the Ruler of the ages,
immortal, invisible, the only wise God,
be honor and glory, through Jesus Christ,
for ever and ever. Amen.

All recite the whole antiphon each day.

ANTIPHON L**IKE THE SUN IN THE MORNING,
THE S**AVIOR OF THE WORLD WILL DAWN.
L**IKE RAIN ON THE MEADOWS HE WILL
 DESCEND.**

Here the Advent Litany (page 16) may be said.

The Lord's Prayer ELLC

Lord, have mercy.
~Christ, have mercy, Lord, have mercy.

Our Father in heaven, (all in unison):
~hallowed be your name,
your kingdom come,
your will be done,
    on earth as in heaven.
Give us today our daily bread.
Forgive us our sins
    as we forgive those who sin against us.
Save us from the time of trial
    and deliver us from evil.
For the kingdom, the power, and the glory
        are yours
    now and for ever. Amen.

Closing Prayers for the Four Weeks of Advent

Stir up your power, O Lord, and come.
Rescue us from the dangers
which threaten us, and be our Savior;
for you are God, living and reigning
        with the Father in the unity of the Holy Spirit,
        forever and ever.
All: ~Amen.

Stir up our hearts, O Lord,
        to prepare Christ's way
        so that through his coming
        we may be worthy to serve you

with our minds made purer;
for you are God, living and reigning
with the Father in the unity of the Holy Spirit,
forever and ever.

All: ~Amen.

Hear our prayers, O Lord,
and enlighten the darkness of our minds
by the grace of your visitation;
for you are God, living and reigning
with the Father in the unity of the Holy Spirit,
forever and ever.

All: ~Amen.

Stir up your power, O Lord, and come,
so that aided by your powerful assistance
we may, through your grace and mercy,
attain your visitation which consoles us now;
for you are God, living and reigning
with the Father in the unity of the Holy Spirit,
forever and ever.

All: ~Amen.

Say to the cities of Judah:
All: ~"Here is your God!"

Blessing

May the Lord Jesus, who is coming in glory
to judge the living and the dead,
† bless us and keep us.

All: ~Amen.

An Advent Litany for Each Day

Leader:

O Wisdom, breath of the Most High,
pervading and controlling all creation
with strength and tenderness:

All: ~Come, and teach us the way of truth.

O Lord of lords and Leader of the house of Israel,
who appeared to Moses in the burning bush
and gave him the Law on Sinai:

~Come, and save us by your mighty arm.

O Flower of Jesse's stock, a signal to the nations;
kings stand mute before you
and all peoples pay you homage:

~Come, deliver us, delay no longer.

O Key of David and Ruler of the house of Israel,
opening the gate of heaven to all believers:

~Come, and set your captive people free.

O Radiant Dawn, splendor of eternal light
and sun of righteousness:

~Come, and shine on those who sit in darkness
and the shadow of death.

O Ruler of all the nations, so long-desired,
the cornerstone of the human household:

~Come and save those whom you have fashioned
from the dust.

All: O Emmanuel, our Ruler and our lawgiver,
  the awaited of the nations and their Savior:
~Come, Lord God, and set us free.

Pause for our special intentions.

O Virgin of virgins, no one like you was ever
  seen before and no one like you will ever appear
    again!
~Come, O Mother of the Word Incarnate,
help us in all our needs.[5]

Advent Prayers at Meals

The Advent Wreath
This wreath is often used in both church and home throughout the whole of Advent. It usually appears on the home altar or the dining room table for all the four weeks of Advent. Four candles, three purple and one pink, are lit gradually as the Sundays appear and pass; two purples for the first two weeks, one pink additional candle for the third week, one final purple added for the fourth week. Most children like to light the Advent candles. The table prayers included here may be the closing prayers for the four weeks.

The leader recites the whole prayer and all answer Amen.

1. Stir up your power, O Lord,
  and come to rescue your Church
  from all the dangers that threaten us

and save us by your great power,
for you live and reign with the Father,
in the unity of the Holy Spirit,
one God, for ever and ever.
~Amen.

2. Stir up our hearts, O Lord,
to prepare the coming
of the Word made flesh
that through his incarnation
the world may be saved
and our minds renewed,
now and for ever.
~Amen.

3. Lord God,
please lend your ears to our petitions
and by the grace of your coming
enlighten the darkness of our minds
that we may serve you in perfect joy;
you live and reign, now and for ever.
~Amen.

4. Stir up your power, O Lord,
and come to rescue us by your great might
that what is hindered by our sins
may be purged by your merciful forgiveness;
you live and reign, now and for ever.
~Amen. [6]

A Novena for Advent

A novena in preparation before Christmas is a traditional custom. It will be a help for those who feel overwhelmed by the secular and business side of our Christmas culture. This devotional novena is a bit briefer than the other devotions in this book.

Christ Jesus † is coming for us;
~Come, let us adore him.

Psalm 117 nab   **Praise God!**

Antiphon Jesus Christ is Lord, *
for the glory of God the Father, alleluia!

Praise the Lord, all you nations!
 Give glory, all you peoples!
The Lord's love for us is strong;
 the Lord is faithful forever.

Antiphon Jesus Christ is Lord,
for the glory of God the Father, alleluia!

Glory to the Father, and to the Son,
 and to the Holy Spirit:
as it was in the beginning, is now,
 and will be for ever. Amen.

Antiphon Jesus Christ is Lord,
for the glory of God the Father, alleluia!

Hymn

Love came down at Christmas,
Love all lovely, Love divine;
Love was born at Christmas,
Star and angels give the sign.

Worship we the Godhead,
Love incarnate, Love divine;
Worship we our Jesus:
But where with for sacred sign?

Love shall be our token,
Love be yours and love be mine.
Love to God and all men,
Love for plea and gift and sign.

Christina Rossetti (1830–1894)[7]

Reading   A Child Born for Us   Isaiah 9:2,6

The people who walked in darkness
   have seen a great light;
those who lived in a land of deep darkness—
   on them light has shined.
For a child has been born for us,
   a son given to us;
authority rests upon his shoulders;
   and he is named
Wonderful Counselor, Mighty God,
   Everlasting Father, Prince of Peace.

Responsory

He shall be called Emmanuel, alleluia!
~He shall be called Emmanuel, alleluia!

God-with-us, alleluia!
~He shall be called Emmanuel, alleluia!

Glory to the Father, and to the Son,
 and to the Holy Spirit:
~He shall be called Emmanuel, alleluia!

Novena Prayer

Word made flesh for our salvation,
incarnate by the Father's will
and the consent of the Virgin Mary:
Be pleased to hear our prayers
as we adore you seated on Mary's lap.

We state our needs.

You promised to hear all those
who pray to the Father in your name.
Hear us and help us and all our children now
In this holy season.
You live and reign with God the Father,
in the unity of the Holy Spirit,
one God, for ever and ever.
~Amen.

May the Christ, the Child of Bethlehem and
 Nazareth,
✝ bless us and keep us.
~Amen.

II
Devotions for Feasts During Advent

The ten devotions in this section mark the preparations for the coming of the Lord Jesus. We begin with the immaculate conception of Mary, continue through the Annunciation, the Visitation, and other Marian feasts, and conclude with a devotion to St. John the Baptist. We also pray devotions in honor of St. Joseph and of St. Nicholas, whose feast falls during Advent. By praying these devotions during Advent, we prepare our hearts for the birth of the savior on Christmas.

December 8
The Immaculate Conception of Mary

After consulting with the wider church, on December 8, 1854, Pope Pius IX published the bull, *Ineffabilis Deus,* which defined the immaculate conception of the Blessed Virgin Mary: "In the first moment of her conception, by the grace and privilege of the merits of Jesus Christ, Savior of the human race, the Virgin Mary was preserved and exempted from all stain of original sin." This means that she was conceived in grace and never sinned in any way for the rest of her life. Like her divine Son she too is a paragon of virtue.

> *She shows us, in the very course of our pilgrimage, what we shall be at that pilgrimage's end—each to our own particular degree—at the moment of humanity's consummation in God. To say that she is the immaculate, does not mean that she did not suffer, that she was never troubled, or that she had no need for faith and hope. She was a daughter of earth, albeit blessed by heaven. She had passions. Everything authentically human was present in her.* [7]

My soul † rejoices in my God
~AND HE HAS ROBED ME IN THE GARMENT OF SALVATION.
The Lord has robed me in the cloak of justice
~LIKE A BRIDE ADORNED WITH HER JEWELS.

PSALM 117 RGP — PRAISE GOD!

ANTIPHON You are the glory of Jerusalem, *
YOU ARE THE BOAST OF ISRAEL,
THE GREAT PRIDE OF OUR NATION, ALLELUIA!

O praise the LORD, all you nations;
acclaim him, all you peoples!
For his merciful love has prevailed over us;
and the LORD's faithfulness endures forever.

ANTIPHON YOU ARE THE GLORY OF JERUSALEM,
YOU ARE THE BOAST OF ISRAEL,
THE GREAT PRIDE OF OUR NATION, ALLELUIA!

Glory to the Father, and to the Son,
 and to the Holy Spirit:
as it was in the beginning, is now,
 and will be for ever. Amen.

ANTIPHON YOU ARE THE GLORY OF JERUSALEM, YOU ARE THE BOAST OF ISRAEL, THE GREAT PRIDE OF OUR NATION, ALLELUIA!

THE CONCEPTION OF OUR LADY

Our second Eve puts on her mortal shroud,
Earth breeds a heaven for God's new dwelling place;
Now rises up Elijah's little cloud,
 That growing shall distill the shower of grace;
Her being now begins, who, ere she end,
Shall bring the good that our evil amend.

Both grace and nature did their force unite
 to make this Babe the sum of all their best;
Our most, her lest, our million, but her mite,
 She was at easiest rate worth all the rest:
What grace to men or angels God did part,
Was all united in this infant's heart.

Four only creatures bred without fault are nam'd,
 And all the rest conceived in sin;
Without both man and wife was Adam fram'd,
 Of man, but not of wife, did Eve begin;
Wife without touch of man Christ's mother was,
Of man and wife this Babe was bred in grace.

St. Robert Southwell, SJ (1561–1595),
English poet and martyr[8]

1. Reading   The Holy City

Revelation 21:1–2,5

I saw a new heaven and a new earth; for the first heaven and the first of earth had passed away, and the sea was no more. And I saw the holy city, the new Jerusalem, coming down out of heaven from God, prepared as a bride adorned for her husband. And the one who was seated on the throne said, "See I am making all things new!"

Pause for quiet prayer.

Responsory

Come, I will show you the bride, the wife of the Lamb.
~Come, I will show you the bride, the wife of the Lamb.

See, I am coming soon, alleluia!
~Come, I will show you the bride, the wife of the Lamb.

Glory to the Father, and to the Son,
and to the Holy Spirit.
~Come, I will show you the bride, the wife of the Lamb.

2. Reading On the Role of the Blessed Virgin in the Plan of Our Salvation

The Father of mercies willed that the Incarnation should be preceded by assent on the part of the predestined mother, so that just as a woman had a share in bringing about death, so also a woman should contribute to life. This is preeminently true of the Mother of Jesus, who gave to the world the life that renews all things, and who was enriched by God with gifts appropriate to such a role. It is no wonder then that it was customary for the holy Fathers to refer to the Mother of God as all holy and free from every sin, as though fashioned by the Holy Spirit and formed as a new creature. Enriched from the first moment of her conception with the splendor of an entirely unique holiness, the Virgin from Nazareth is hailed by the heralding angel, by divine command, as "full of grace" (Luke 1:28), and to the heavenly messenger she replies: "Behold the handmaid of the Lord, be it done to me according to your word" (Luke 1:38). Thus the daughter of Adam, consenting to the word of God, became the Mother of Jesus. Committing herself wholeheartedly to God's saving will and impeded by no sin, she devoted herself, whole-heartedly to God's saving will and impeded by no sin, she devoted herself totally as a handmaid of the Lord, to the person and work of her Son, under and with him, serving the mystery of redemption, by the grace of Almighty God.[9]

Pause for quiet prayer.

Responsory

Blessed is the fruit of your womb, alleluia!
~Blessed is the fruit of your womb, alleluia!

You are all holy and free from all sin, alleluia!
~BLESSED IS THE FRUIT OF YOUR WOMB,
    ALLELUIA!

Glory to the Father, and to the Son,
  and to the Holy Spirit.
~BLESSED IS THE FRUIT OF YOUR WOMB, ALLELUIA!

THE CANTICLE OF THE VIRGIN MARY   LUKE 1:46–55ELLC

ANTIPHON You are all fair, O Mary, *
    AND NO STAIN OF SIN MARS YOUR LOVELINESS,
        ALLELUIA!

My soul † proclaims the greatness of the Lord,
my spirit rejoices in God my Savior,
for you, Lord, have looked with favor on your
        lowly servant.
From this day all generations will call me blessed:
  you, the Almighty, have done great things for me
  and holy is your name.
  You have mercy on those who fear you
  from generation to generation.
You have shown strength with your arm
and scattered the proud in their conceit,
casting down the mighty from their thrones
and lifting up the lowly.
You have filled the hungry with good things
and sent the rich away empty.
You have come to the aid of your servant Israel,
to remember the promise of mercy,

the promise made to our forebears,
to Abraham and his children for ever.

Glory to the Holy and Undivided Trinity:
now and always, and for ever and ever. Amen.

ANTIPHON YOU ARE ALL FAIR, O MARY,
   AND NO STAIN OF SIN MARS YOUR LOVELINESS,
   ALLELUIA!

THE LORD'S PRAYER
Lord, have mercy.
~CHRIST, HAVE MERCY. LORD, HAVE MERCY.

Our Father in heaven, (all in unison):

CLOSING PRAYER
Father of all holiness,
by the foreseen merits of Jesus her Son,
you created Mary in grace,
even at the first moment of her conception.
By her unceasing intercession,
may the Church be holy and without blemish
and stand rejoicing in your sight
when Christ comes again in glory
to judge the living and the dead.
We ask this through the same Christ our Lord.
~AMEN.

From this day all generations will call me blessed,
   alleluia!
~YOU, THE ALMIGHTY, HAVE DONE GREAT THINGS
   FOR ME, ALLELUIA!

BLESSING

By the merits and prayers of Mary Immaculate,
may the Lord ✝ bring us into our heavenly home.
~AMEN.

THE MOST PURE VIRGIN AND MOTHER OF GOD

Come, let us dance in the Spirit!
Let us sing worthy praises to Christ!
Let us celebrate the joy of Joachim and Anna,
The conception of the Mother of God,
For she is the fruit of the grace of God.

Anna besought the Lord in fervent prayer for
    a child.
The voice of the angel proclaimed to her:
God has granted you the desire of your prayer.
Do not weep, for you shall be a fruitful vine,
Bearing the wondrous branch of the Virgin
Who will bring forth in the flesh the blossom
    of Christ,
Who grants great mercy to the world.

Today the great mercy of all eternity,
Whose depths angels and humans cannot perceive,
Appears in the barren womb of Anna.
Mary the Maiden of God, is prepared to be
  the dwelling place of the eternal King
Who will renew human nature.
Let us entreat her with a pure heart and say:
Intercede for us with your Son and God
That our souls may be saved.[10]

The Nativity of the Virgin Mary

At the time of Mary's birth, Israel was steeped in darkness, either collaborating with pagan Rome or violently revolting against Roman power. Jesus the Messiah takes the way of nonviolence. Mary, his chosen mother, was the new Eve of the new covenant of her Son's way to justice and peace. She was born in the darkness of her time but came without sin, in the holiness of the new order.

A Byzantine Troparion

Your Nativity, O Mother of God, heralded joy to the whole universe, for from you arose the Sun of Justice, Christ our God. He canceled the curse and poured forth his grace: He vanquished death and granted us eternal life.[11]

Let us celebrate ✝ the birth of the Virgin Mary,
~WHO BROUGHT LIFE AND LIGHT INTO THE WORLD.
You are the sun of righteousness,
~O CHRIST OUR LORD.

PSALM 117 RGP   **PRAISE GOD!**

ANTIPHON Your nativity, O Mother of God, *
IS THE ORNAMENT OF ALL THE CHURCHES,
ALLELUIA!

O praise the LORD, all you nations;
acclaim him, all you peoples!
For his merciful love has prevailed over us;
and the LORD's faithfulness endures forever.

Antiphon Your nativity, O Mother of God,
   is the ornament of all the churches,
      alleluia!

Glory to the Father, and to the Son,
  and to the Holy Spirit:
as it was in the beginning, is now,
  and will be for ever. Amen.

Antiphon Your nativity, O Mother of God,
   is the ornament of all the churches,
      alleluia!

2. Our Lady's Nativity

Joy in the rising of our orient star,
That shall bring forth the Sun that lent her light;
Joy in the peace that shall conclude our war,
And soon rebate the edge of Satan's spite;
Lodestar of all engulfed in worldly waves,
The card and compass that from shipwreck saves.

The patriarch and prophets were the flowers
Which time by course of ages did distill,
And culled into this little cloud the showers
Whose gracious drops the world with joy shall fill;
Whose moisture fills up every soul with grace,
And brings life to Adam's dying race.

For on earth, she is the royal throne,
The chosen cloth to make his mortal weed;
The quarry to cut out our Cornerstone,
Soil full of fruit, yet free from mortal seed;

For heavenly Flower she is the Jesse rod
The child of man, the parent of a God.

> St. Robert Southwell, SJ (1561–1595),
> English poet and martyr[12]

THE CANTICLE OF JUDITH THE VALIANT
13:18–20; 15:9 TEV

ANTIPHON The Almighty has done great things for you *

AND HOLY IS YOUR NAME, ALLELUIA!

The Most High God has blessed you
  more than any woman on earth.
How worthy of praise is the Lord God
  who created heaven and earth!
He guided you as you cut off the head
  of our deadliest enemy.

Your trust in God will never be forgotten
to those who tell of God's power.
May God give you everlasting honor
for what you have done.

May he reward you with blessings
because you remained faithful to him.
And did not hesitate to risk your own life
to relieve the oppression of your people.

You are Jerusalem's crowning glory,
the heroine of Israel,
the pride and joy of your people.

ANTIPHON THE ALMIGHTY HAS DONE GREAT THINGS FOR YOU AND HOLY IS YOUR NAME, ALLELUIA!

PRAYER

Let us pray (pause for silent prayer):

Holy Mother of God,
like Judith of old,
you ventured everything
and became the pride and joy
of your holy people.
Bring us home at last, dear Mother,
to the throne of glory prepared for us
from the foundation of the world.
You live and reign with your divine Son,
now and for ever.
~AMEN.

1. READING **MARY'S ANCESTRY** **MATTHEW 1:1–2, 5–6,16**

An account of the genealogy of Jesus the Messiah, the son of David, the son of Abraham. Abraham was the father of Isaac, and Isaac the father of Jacob, and Jacob the father of Judah and his brothers, . . . and Obed the father of Jesse, and Jesse the father of King David. And David the father of Solomon by the wife of Uriah, . . . And Jacob the father of Joseph, the husband of Mary, of whom Jesus was born, who is called the Messiah.

Pause for quiet prayer.

Responsory

Great Mother of God, your birth brings joy
   to the whole universe.
~Great Mother of God, your birth
      brings joy
   to the whole universe.

Your life illuminates the whole Church, alleluia!
~Great Mother of God, your birth
      brings joy
   to the whole universe.

Glory to the Father, and to the Son,
   and to the Holy Spirit:
~Great Mother of God, your birth
      brings joy
   to the whole universe.

2. A Reading from Saint Augustine of Hippo Regius:

The much desired feast of Blessed Mary ever Virgin has come; so let our land illumined by such a birth, be glad with greatest rejoicing. For she is the flower of the field from whom blossomed the precious Lily of the valley, through whose birth that nature inherited from our first parents is changed and guilt is blotted out. Eve mourned, Mary rejoiced. Eve carried tears in her heart; Mary, joy. For Eve gave birth to sinners, Mary to the Innocent One. Eve struck, and Mary healed. Disobedience is displaced by obedience, and fidelity atones for infidelity. Now let Mary play upon musical instruments and let timbrels reverberate under the fleet fingers of this young Mother. Let joyous choirs sing together harmoniously, and let sweet songs be blended now with one melody and now with another. Hear now how our timbrel player has sung. For she sang: "My soul proclaims the greatness of the Lord, my spirit rejoices in God my Savior, for you, Lord, have looked with favor on your lowly servant. For this day all generations will call me blessed." This miraculous new birth has utterly vanquished the root of aimless wanderings; Mary's canticle has ended the lamentations of Eve.

St. Augustine of Hippo Regius (354–430)[13]

Pause for quiet prayer.

Responsory

I grew tall like a cedar in Lebanon, alleluia!
~I grew tall like a cedar in Lebanon, alleluia!

And like a cypress on the heights of Hermon.
~I grew tall like a cedar in Lebanon, alleluia!

Glory to the Father, and to the Son,
  and to the Holy Spirit:
~I grew tall like a cedar in Lebanon, alleluia!

The Lord's Prayer

Lord, have mercy.
~Christ, have mercy. Lord, have mercy.

Our Father in heaven, (all in unison):

Closing Prayer

Father of mercy,
the birth of Mary's Son
was the dawn of our salvation.
May this celebration of her birthday
bring us closer to lasting peace.
We ask this through Christ our Lord.
~Amen.

God made you more beautiful than the sun,
    alleluia!
~And every constellation of the stars,
    alleluia!

Blessing

By the prayers of the Blessed Virgin Mary,
may Almighty God bless us,
the Father, ✝ the Son, and the Holy Spirit.
~Amen.

Mary's Presentation in the Temple

According to two legends of the second century, when Mary was three years of age, Joachim and Anna presented her to the temple so that she might be consecrated to the Lord. They invited the young girls of the city to walk before her with lighted torches and as soon as they reached the temple, Mary unhesitatingly went up the steps of the sanctuary where she was to remain until she was espoused to Joseph of Nazareth.

At the Lete

*Behold the day of joy the most
venerable season are here!
For the one who was a virgin before
giving birth
remained a perfect virgin, even after she
gave birth.
She is presented today in the holy Temple
to the admiration of the High Priest.
Let Joachim rejoice and Anna dance
with glee,
for they have presented to God
the Lady Immaculate and all blameless,
when she was only three years old.
O Mothers, rejoice! You virgins, be merry!
Barren women,
share your happiness! Rejoice, O nations of
the world, and be glad!*[14]

Let us celebrate ✝ this holy day!
~Let us honor the Virgin Mother of God! Today she is presented to the Temple of the Lord

~For she has been chosen from among all generations.

Hymn

God who made the earth and sky
And the changing sea,
Clothed his glory in our flesh,
One with us to be.

Mary, Virgin filled with light,
Chosen from our race,
Bore the Father's only Son
By the Spirit's grace.

He whom nothing can contain,
No one can compel,
Bound his timeless Godhead here,
In our time to dwell.

God, our Father, Lord of days,
And his only Son,
With the Holy Spirit praise:
Trinity in One.[15]

Psalm 98   Victory to Our God

Antiphon Your holy Child, Mary, *
will be called the Son of God, alleluia!

O sing to the Lord a new song,
   for the Lord has done marvelous things!
God's right hand and holy arm
   have gotten victory.

The Lord has declared victory,
  and has revealed vindication in the sight
    of the nations.
The Lord has remembered steadfast love
    and faithfulness
  to the house of the Lord.
All the ends of the earth have seen
  the victory of our God.

Make a joyful noise to the Lord, all the earth;
  break forth into joyous song and sing praises!
Sing praises to the Lord with the lyre,
  with the lyre and the sound of melody!
With trumpets and the sound of the horn
  make a joyful noise before the Ruler, the Lord!

Let the sea roar, and all that fears it;
  the world and those who dwell in it!
Let the floods clap their hands;
  let the hills sing for joy together before the Lord,
who comes to judge the earth.
  The Lord will judge the world with
        righteousness,
    and the peoples with equity.

Antiphon Your holy Child, Mary,
will be called the Son of God, alleluia!

Psalm Prayer

Let us pray (pause for quiet payer):

Chosen Mother of the Messiah,

tabernacle of the Most High God:
Be with our pilgrimage through life
and favor us with your prayers
until we overcome death
by the grace of your Son Jesus,
the Savior of the world.
~AMEN.

1. READING   **CLOUD AND FIRE**   **EXODUS 40:1–3,34–35**

The Lord spoke to Moses: On the first day of the first month you shall set up the tabernacle of the tent of meeting. You shall put in it the ark of the covenant, and you shall screen the ark with the curtain. Then the cloud covered the tent of meeting and the glory of the LORD filled the tabernacle. Moses was not able to enter the tent of meeting because the cloud settled upon it, and the glory of the LORD filled the tabernacle.

Pause for quiet prayer.

RESPONSORY

Moses put the golden altar in the Tent,
~MOSES PUT THE GOLDEN ALTAR IN THE TENT,

And burned sweet-smelling incense on it.
~MOSES PUT THE GOLDEN ALTAR IN THE TENT,

Glory to the Father, and to the Son,
  and to the Holy Spirit:
~MOSES PUT THE GOLDEN ALTAR IN THE TENT.

2. Reading from the Proto-Gospel of James: The Presentation

When the child [Mary] turned three, Joachim said, "We shall call the undefiled daughters of the Hebrews and have each take a torch and set them up, blazing, that the child not turn back and her heart be taken captive away from the Temple of the Lord." They did this, until they had gone up to the Lord's Temple. And the priest of the Lord received her and gave her a kiss, blessing her and saying, "The Lord has made your name great among all generations. Through you will the Lord reveal his redemption to the sons of Israel at the end of time."

He set her on the third step of the altar, and the Lord God cast his grace down upon her. She danced on her feet, and the entire house of Israel loved her.[16]

Pause for quiet prayer.

Responsory

The Temple was filled with smoke, alleluia!
~THE TEMPLE WAS FILLED WITH SMOKE, ALLELUIA!

From the glory and power of God, alleluia!
~THE TEMPLE WAS FILLED WITH SMOKE, ALLELUIA!

Glory to the Father, and to the Son,
  and to the Holy Spirit:
~THE TEMPLE WAS FILLED WITH SMOKE,
  ALLELUIA!

A CANTICLE OF ISAIAH THE PROPHET 52:7–10

ANTIPHON You have done great things for me *
AND HOLY IS YOUR NAME.

How beautiful upon the mountains
  are the feet of the messenger who announces
      peace,
who brings good news,
  who announces salvation,
  who says to Zion, "Your God reigns."

Listen! Your sentinels lift up their voices,
  together they sing for joy!
for in plain sight they see
  the return of the LORD to Zion.

Break forth together into singing,
  you ruins of Jerusalem;
for the LORD has comforted his people,
  he has redeemed Jerusalem.

The LORD has bared his holy arm
  before the eyes of all the nations;
and all the ends of the earth shall see
  the salvation of our God.

ANTIPHON YOU HAVE DONE GREAT THINGS FOR ME
AND HOLY IS YOUR NAME.

The Lord's Prayer
Lord, have mercy.
~Christ, have mercy. Lord, have mercy.
Our Father in heaven, (all in unison):

Closing Prayer
Most High God,
you inspired Joachim and Anna
to present their precious child
in the Temple of the God of Israel.
May the merits and prayers of the Virgin Mary,
be found worthy to be the presented to your glory
for us and your whole Church,
now and for ever.
~Amen.

Stir up your might, O Lord;
~And come to save us.

Blessing
May Mary, the Virgin of virgins,
† intercede with the Lord.
~Amen.

December 6
Saint Nicholas of Myra in Lycia

St. Nicholas lived in the fourth century. He was a zealous bishop and a wonderworker. He was imprisoned during the great persecution of Emperor Diocletian and participated in the Ecumenical Council of Nicea in

325 where he denounced Arius and his false teachings about the Son of God. His hard work and his care for children and sailors inspired legends that increased his popularity, especially in Greece, Russia, and Sicily. In the Netherlands he became the patron (Sint Klaes, Santa Claus) of children and sponsored gift-giving on his feast day. Dutch settlers brought this custom to North America.

Nicholas † was a great priest
~Who in his time pleased God.
He was a great wonderworker of miracles
~And a model of Christian charity.

Psalm 117 RGP   Praise God!

Antiphon The Lord conducted Nicholas *
and showed him the kingdom of God.

O praise the Lord, all you nations;
acclaim him, all you peoples!
For his merciful love has prevailed over us;
and the Lord's faithfulness endures forever.

Antiphon The Lord conducted Nicholas
and showed him the kingdom of God.

Glory to the Father, and to the Son,
   and to the Holy Spirit:
as it was in the beginning, is now,
   and will be for ever. Amen.

Antiphon The Lord conducted Nicholas
and showed him the kingdom of God.

Hymn

Blest are the pure in heart,
For they shall see our God,
The secret of the Lord is theirs,
Their soul is God's abode.

The Lord who left the heavens
Our life and peace to bring,
To dwell in lowliness on earth,
Our pattern and our king.

Still to the lowly soul
He does himself impart
And for his dwelling and his throne
Chooses the pure in heart.

Lord we your presence seek;
May ours this blessing be;
Give us a pure and lowly heart.
A temple meet for thee.

> John Keble (1792–1866) and
> William John Hall (1793–1861)[17]

Psalm 40: 4–5,7–9 RGP Great Is the Lord

Antiphon My lips I have not sealed *
  you know it, O Lord.

He put a new song into my mouth,
praise of our God.
Many shall see and fear
and shall trust in the Lord.

Blessed the man who has placed
his trust in the Lord,
and has not gone over to the proud
who follow false gods.

You delight not in sacrifice and offerings,
but in an open ear.
You do not ask for holocaust and victim.

Then I said, "See, I have come."
In the scroll of the book it stands written of me:
"I delight to do your will, O my God;
your instruction lies deep within me."

Antiphon My lips I have not sealed
you know it, O Lord.

Psalm Prayer

Let us pray (pause for quiet prayer):

Good Shepherd of the sheep:
Raise up new pastors in your Church
like the good Bishop Nicholas
that we may serve the Lord Christ
as he did in love and service of his people.
We ask this through Christ our Lord.
~Amen.

1. Reading   **Servants of God**   **1 Timothy 6:11–15**

Man of God, pursue righteousness, godliness,
faith, love, endurance, gentleness. Fight the
good fight of the faith; take hold of eternal life,
to which you were called and for which you

were made the good confession in the presence of many witnesses. In the presence of God, who gives life to all things, and of Christ Jesus, who in his testimony before Pontius Pilate made the confession, I charge you to keep the commandment without spot or blame until the manifestation of our Lord Jesus Christ, which he will bring about at the right time—he who is the blessed and only Sovereign, the King of kings and Lord of lords.

Pause for quiet prayer.

Responsory

God sent Nicholas to bring good news to the poor,
~God sent Nicholas to bring good news to the poor,

And freedom to prisoners and children, alleluia!
~God sent Nicholas to bring good news to the poor,

Glory to the Father, and to the Son,
 and to the Holy Spirit:
~God sent Nicholas to bring good news to the poor.

2. A Reading from the Golden Legend of James de Varagine, OP (ca. 1230–1298):

Nicholas was born in the famous city of Patara in Lycia. His birth was an answer to his parents' prayers. Having lost his parents when he was a young man, he gave all his goods to the poor. Here is an example of his Christian charity: It so happened that his neighbor had three virgin daughters, but being too poor to obtain them an honorable marriage, he was constrained to abandon them to prostitution in order to survive. When the holy man Nicholas discovered this, he secretly threw a sum of money into their home by night. When the neighbor discovered this gift, he provided a dowry for his eldest daughter. In the following nights Nicholas repeated this on two other occasions and so saved them from prostitution.[18]

Pause for quiet prayer.

Responsory

Nicholas worked great wonders before God, alleluia!

~Nicholas worked great wonders before God, alleluia!

May he intercede for the needs of all, alleluia!

~Nicholas worked great wonders before God, alleluia!

Glory to the Father, and to the Son,
 and to the Holy Spirit:

~Nicholas worked great wonders before God, alleluia!

The Lord's Prayer

Lord, have mercy.

~CHRIST, HAVE MERCY. LORD, HAVE MERCY.

Our Father in heaven, (all in unison):

Closing Prayer

Father,
hear our prayers for mercy,
and by the help of Saint Nicholas
keep us safe from all danger,
and guide us on the way of salvation.
Please grant this through Christ our Lord.
~AMEN.
You have filled the hungry with good things,
    alleluia!
~AND SENT THE RICH AWAY EMPTY, ALLELUIA!

Blessing

By the prayers of blessed Nicholas the wonder
    worker
✝ may Christ the Lord bless and keep us.
~AMEN.

December 12
Our Lady of Guadalupe

Mary's most significant apparition in the New World was in December 1531 at Tepeyac, just outside Mexico City, to Juan Diego, a poor campesino who had recently converted to Christianity. Her message was one of compassion for the conquered peoples of Central

America. She appeared speaking their language, dressed in their sacred colors, and as a mestizo, the Dark Virgin, the Apostle of the native peoples, and Mother of the Americas. This thoroughly American feast of Mary is very appropriate to Advent just after her immaculate conception, the very beginning of her life.

Blessed are you † among women, O Mary,
~And blessed is the fruit of your womb,
 Jesus.
You are more honorable than the cherubim,
~And far more exalted than the seraphim!

Hymn

The ark which God has sanctified,
Which he has filled with grace,
Within the temple of the Lord
Has found a resting place.

More glorious than the seraphim,
This ark of love divine;
Corruption could not blemish her
Whom death could not confine.

God-bearing Mother, virgin chaste,
Who shines in heaven's sight,
She wears a royal crown of stars
Who is the door of light.

To Father, Son, and Spirit blest
May we give endless praise
With Mary, who is queen of heaven,
Through everlasting days.[19]

PSALM 121 — THE MOTHER OF CHRIST

ANTIPHON A flower has sprung from Jesse's root; *
A STAR HAS RISEN OUT OF JACOB,
A VIRGIN HAS BROUGHT FORTH THE SAVIOR.

I lift up my eyes to the hills—
 from where does my help come?
My help comes from the LORD,
 who made heaven and earth.
The LORD will not let your foot be moved,
 the LORD who keeps you will not slumber.
The One who keeps Israel
 will neither slumber nor sleep.

The LORD is your keeper;
 the LORD is your shade on your right hand.
The sun shall not strike you by day,
 nor the moon by night.

The LORD will keep you from all evil,
 and will keep your life.

The LORD will keep your going out
 and your coming in
 from this time forth and for evermore. Amen

ANTIPHON A FLOWER HAS SPRUNG FROM JESSE'S ROOT;
A STAR HAS RISEN OUT OF JACOB:
A VIRGIN HAS BROUGHT FORTH THE SAVIOR.

Psalm Prayer

Let us pray (pause for silent prayer):

Holy Mother of God,
you conceived in your womb
the One whom the whole world cannot contain.
By your loving intercession,
help us build up the Church,
sustain our families,
and strengthen our friendships,
by the redeeming power of Christ our Savior.
~Amen.

1. Reading   **The Seat of Wisdom**   **Sirach 24:19–22**

Come to me, you who desire me, and eat your fill of my fruits. For the memory of me is sweeter than honey, and the possession of me sweeter than the honeycomb. Those who eat of me will hunger for more, and those who drink of me will thirst for more. Whoever obeys me will not be put to shame, and those who work with me will not sin.

Pause for quiet prayer.

Responsory

My spirit rejoices in God my Savior, alleluia!
~My spirit rejoices in God my Savior, alleluia!

For all generations will call me blessed, alleluia!
~My spirit rejoices in God my Savior, alleluia!

Glory to the Father, and to the Son,
  And to the Holy Spirit:
~My spirit rejoices in God my Savior,
    alleluia!

2. A Reading from the Nican Mopohua:

The Mother of God conversed with Juan Diego and unveiled her precious will: "Know and be certain in your heart, my most abandoned son, that I am the Ever-Virgin Holy Mary, Mother of God of Great Truth, Teotl, of the One through Whom We Live, the Creator of Persons, the Owner of What is Near and Together, of the Lord of heaven and earth.

I very much want and ardently desire that my hermitage be erected in this place. In it I will show and give to all people all my love, my compassion, my help, and my protection, because I am your merciful mother and the mother of all the nations that live on this earth, who would love me, who would speak with me, who would search for me, and who would place their confidence in me. I will hear their laments and remedy and cure all their miseries, misfortunes, and sorrows."[20]

Pause for quiet prayer.

Responsory

You cast down the mighty from their thrones.
~You cast down the mighty from their
    thrones.

And lift up the lowly, alleluia!
~You cast down the mighty from their
    thrones.

Glory to the Father, and to the Son,
  and to the Holy Spirit:
~You cast down the mighty from their
    thrones.

A Canticle of   **61:10–11;**
Isaiah the Prophet   **62:1,3**

Antiphon God makes her shine * like a burning torch,

alleluia!

I will greatly rejoice in the Lord,
  my whole being shall exult in my God;
for he has clothed me with the garments of
        salvation,
  and he has covered me with the robe of
        righteousness,
as a bridegroom decks himself with a garland,
  and as a bride adorns herself with her jewels.

For as the earth brings forth its shoots
  and as a garden causes what is sown in it to
        spring up,
so the Lord God will cause righteousness and
        praise
  to spring up before all the nations.

For Zion's sake I will not keep silent,
  and for Jerusalem's sake I will not rest,

until her vindication shines out like the dawn,
  and her salvation like a burning torch.
You shall be a crown of beauty in the hand of the
    Lord,
  and a royal diadem in the hand of your God.

To the Ruler of the ages,
  immortal, invisible, the only wise God,
be honor and glory, through Jesus Christ,
  for ever and ever. Amen.

Antiphon God makes her shine like a burning torch,
  alleluia!

A Marian Litany

Lord Jesus Christ, Son of God and Son of Mary:
~Have mercy on us.

Lord Jesus Christ, who was born in Bethlehem
  of Judea:
~Have mercy on us.

Lord Jesus Christ, who lived in obedience
  to Mary and Joseph at Nazareth:
~Have mercy on us.

Lord Jesus Christ, whose mother stood mourning
  at the foot of the cross:
~Have mercy on us.

Lord Jesus Christ, who commended your mother
  to your beloved disciple:
~Have mercy on us.

Lord Jesus Christ, who assumed your mother
body and soul into the glory of heaven:
~HAVE MERCY ON US.

Lord Jesus Christ, who wants your mother to be
revered in every generation and by every people:
~HAVE MERCY ON US.

Pause for our special intentions.

Commemorating our most holy and glorious
Lady, the Ever Virgin Mary and Mother of
God, Saint Juan Diego, and all the saints, let us
commend ourselves, each other, and our whole
life with Christ our God.
~TO YOU, O LORD.

THE LORD'S PRAYER
Lord, have mercy.
~CHRIST, HAVE MERCY. LORD, HAVE MERCY.
Our Father in heaven, (all in unison):

CLOSING PRAYER
Holy Mother of God, and Queen of heaven,
at Tepeyac you promised to show
all the nations of the earth
your love, compassion, help, and protection.
Because you are our merciful Mother,
hear our laments, and remedy all our miseries,
    misfortunes, and sorrows.
Stamp your priceless image on our hearts,
unveil your precious will for us,

and hold us in the hollow of your mantle
where you cross your arms,
now and for ever.
~Amen.

Blessing

May Holy Mary, Mother of the Americas,
† be the joy and consolation of her people.
~Amen.

The Espousals of Mary and Joseph

It is believed that when Mary left the precincts of the temple, she was espoused to Joseph of Nazareth at thirteen or fourteen years of age. Mary probably had already taken a vow of virginity, but Gabriel's message changed everything, except for her virginity. Perhaps Joseph made a vow of virginity too, but in all events they were legally married but remained in perfect chastity.

Hail, holy Parent, † that brought forth the King *
~Who rules heaven and earth for ever and ever.
He whom the whole world cannot contain.
~Enclosed himself in your virginal womb.

Psalm 117 RGP   Praise God!

Antiphon Come, let us adore the King of kings, *
  Jesus, the Son of Mary!

O praise the Lord, all you nations;
acclaim him, all you peoples!

For his merciful love has prevailed over us;
and the Lord's faithfulness endures forever.

Antiphon Come, let us adore the King of kings, Jesus, the Son of Mary!

Glory to the Father, and to the Son,
  and to the Holy Spirit:
as it was in the beginning, is now,
~and will be for ever. Amen.

Antiphon Come, let us adore the King of kings, Jesus, the Son of Mary!

Our Lady's Spousals

Wife did she live, yet virgin did she die,
  Untouched of man, yet mother of a son;
To save herself and child from fatal lie,
  To end the web whereof the thread was spun,
In marriage knots to Joseph she was tied,
Unwonted works with wonted veils to hide.

God lent his paradise to Joseph's care,
  Wherein he was to plant the tree of life;
His Son, of Joseph's child the title bare,
  Just cause to make the mother Joseph's wife.
O blessed man! betrothed to such a spouse,
More blest to live with such a child in house!

No carnal love this sacred league procured,
  All vain delights were far from their assent;
Though both in wedlock bands themselves assured,

Yet straight by vow they sealed their chaste
> intent:
Thus had she virgins', wives', and widows' crown,
And by chaste childbirth doubled her renown.

> St. Robert Southwell, SJ (1561–1595),
> English poet and martyr[21]

Psalm 45:11–18 RGP   The Virgin of Virgins

Antiphon Holy and immaculate Virgin *
YOU ARE ESPOUSED WITH RIGHTEOUS JOSEPH,
THE FOSTER FATHER OF JESUS, ALLELUIA!

Listen, O daughter; pay heed and give ear:
forget your own people and your father's house.
So will the King desire your beauty.
He is your LORD, pay your homage to him.

And the daughter of Tyre shall come with gifts;
the richest of the people shall seek your favor.
The daughter of the king is clothed with splendor;
her robes are threaded with gold.

In fine clothing she is led to the king;
behind her are her maiden companions, brought
> to you.
They are escorted amid gladness and joy;
they pass within the palace of the king.

Sons will be yours to succeed your fathers;
you will make them rulers over all the earth.
I will make your name forever remembered.
Thus the peoples will praise you from age to age.

Antiphon Holy and immaculate Virgin you are espoused with righteous Joseph, the foster father of Jesus, alleluia!

Psalm Prayer

Let us pray (pause for quiet prayer):

Holy Mary and Joseph,
united in marriage and parents of Jesus:
Help us in holy wedlock
to share the gifts of God
through a lifetime together in love and peace,
now and for ever.

~Amen.

1. Reading — **Mary Is Espoused to Joseph** — **Matthew 1:18–21**

When his mother Mary had been engaged to Joseph, but before they lived together, she was found to be with child from the Holy Spirit. Her husband Joseph, being a righteous man and unwilling to expose her to public disgrace, planned to dismiss her quietly. But just when he had resolved to do this an angel of the Lord appeared to him in a dream and said, "Joseph, son of David, do not be afraid to take Mary as your wife, for the child conceived in her is from the Holy Spirit. She will bear a son, and you are to name him Jesus, for he will save his people from their sins."

Pause for quiet prayer.

Responsory

Blest are you, O Virgin Mary, the Mother of God!
~Blest are you, O Virgin Mary, the Mother of God!

By God's gift, you were married to Joseph of Nazareth.
~Blest are you, O Virgin Mary, the Mother of God!

Glory to the Father, and to the Son,
and to the Holy Spirit:
~Blest are you, O Virgin Mary, the Mother of God!

2. A Reading from a Homily of Saint John of Damascus:

An angel announced the conception of her [Mary] who was to be born. For in this respect, too, it was right that she who was to be the bearer, in flesh, of the sole and truly perfect God should not be lacking anything, or take second place. She was later consecrated in the holy temple of God and lived there, displaying a better and purer ideal and way of life than others, free from all contact with immoral men and women. But when the bloom of maturity came upon her, and the law forbade her to remain within the sacred precincts, she was betrothed to a suitor who was to be, properly speaking, the guardian of her virginity: Joseph, from the ranks of priests, who until his old age

had kept the law without compromise, far better
than his peers. This holy and spotless maiden now
lived with him, remaining at home and knowing
nothing of what transpired outside her doors.

St. John of Damascus
(ca. 675–ca. 749)[22]

Pause for quiet prayer.

Responsory
He shall be called Emmanuel, God-is-with-us!
~He shall be called Emmanuel,
   God-is-with-us!

The Word was made flesh and dwelt among us.
~He shall be called Emmanuel,
   God-is-with-us!

Glory to the Father, and to the Son,
  and to the Holy Spirit:
~He shall be called Emmanuel,
   God-is-with-us!

The Lord's Prayer
Lord, have mercy.
~Christ, have mercy. Lord, have mercy.

Our Father in heaven (all in unison):

Closing Prayer
Grant your servants, O Lord,
the gift of heavenly grace
so that the childbearing of the Virgin Mary

The Espousals of Mary and Joseph

be the beginning of our salvation,
and so that the feast of her espousals
may bring us greater peace and joy.
We ask this through Christ our Lord.
~Amen.

God, your God, has anointed you, alleluia!
~With the oil of gladness above your peers,
    alleluia!

Blessing
May the Virgin Mary mild
† bless us with her holy Child.
~Amen.

The Third Wednesday of Advent
The Annunciation of the Lord

After the Councils of Ephesus (431) and Chalcedon (451), devotion to the mother of God (Theotokos) spread like wildfire across the Catholic world. It multiplied the discovery of her relics, the founding of churches, shrines, pilgrimages, the creation of feasts, hymns, prayers, and sermons in exaltation of the incarnation of Christ and of his Virgin Mother.

One of the first of the new feasts was that of the Annunciation: God sent the archangel Gabriel to the Blessed Virgin Mary, bringing the good news of the Incarnation, and Mary gave her free consent to God's initiative (Luke 1:26–56). This feast appeared first in the fifth century, in the east Roman Empire, spread to Old Rome in the late seventh century, and ultimately, to all the churches of East and West. It was sometimes held in December and sometimes on March 25.

Hail, Mary, ☩ bright star that bore the Sun.
~HAIL, MARY, CHRIST'S WONDERS NOW BEGUN.
Hail, Mary, marvel sung of angel hosts.
~HAIL, MARY, WISDOM OF THE WISE SURPASSING.
Hail, Mary, of faith the firm foundation.
~HAIL, MARY, OF GRACE THE SHINING TOKEN.[23]

PSALM 117 RGP — PRAISE GOD AND MARY!

ANTIPHON You are the glory of Jerusalem, *
 YOU ARE THE BOAST OF ISRAEL,
 THE GREAT PRIDE OF OUR NATION, ALLELUIA!

O praise the LORD, all you nations;
acclaim him, all you peoples!
For his merciful love has prevailed over us;
and the LORD's faithfulness endures forever.

ANTIPHON YOU ARE THE GLORY OF JERUSALEM,
 YOU ARE THE BOAST OF ISRAEL,
 THE GREAT PRIDE OF OUR NATION, ALLELUIA!

Glory to the Father, and to the Son,
 and to the Holy Spirit:
as it was in the beginning, is now,
~AND WILL BE FOR EVER. AMEN.

ANTIPHON YOU ARE THE GLORY OF JERUSALEM,
 YOU ARE THE BOAST OF ISRAEL,
 THE GREAT PRIDE OF OUR NATION, ALLELUIA!

Our Lady's Salutation

Spell Eva back and Ave shall you find,
The first began, the last reversed our harm,
An angel's witching words did Eva blind,
An angel's Ave disenchants the charms;
Death first by woman's weakness entered in,
In woman's virtue life does now begin.

O Virgin breast! the heavens to you incline,
In you their joy and sovereign recognize;
Too mean their glory is to match with thine
Whose chaste receipt God more than heaven
      did prize.
Hail, fairest heaven that heaven and earth did bless,
Where virtue's star God's Son of justice is.

With haughty mind to Godhead man aspired,
And was by pride from place of pleasure chased;
With loving mind our manhead God desired,
And us by love in greater pleasure placed;
Man laboring to ascend, procured our fall,
God yielding to descend, cut off our thrall.

St. Robert Southwell, SJ (1561–1595),
English poet and martyr[24]

Psalm 46 RGP   God Is with Us

Antiphon Mary is the city of God, *
   the holy dwelling of the Most High.

God is our refuge and strength,
an ever-present help in distress:
so we shall not fear though the earth should rock,

though mountains quake to the heart of the sea;
even though its waters rage and foam,
even though the mountains be shaken by its tumult.

The Lord of host is with us:
the God of Jacob is our stronghold.
The waters of a river give joy to God's city,
the holy place, the dwelling of the Most High.
God is within, it cannot be shaken;
God will help it at the dawning of the day.
Nations are in tumult, kingdoms are shaken:
he lifts his voice, the earth melts away.

The Lord of hosts is with us:
the God of Jacob is our stronghold.

Come and behold the works of the Lord,
the awesome deeds he has done on the earth.
He puts an end to wars over all the earth;
the bow he breaks, the spear he snaps, the shields
    he burns with fire:
"Be still and know that I am God,
exalted over nations, exalted over earth!"

The Lord of hosts is with us:
the God of Jacob is our stronghold.

Antiphon Mary is the city of God,
the holy dwelling of the Most High.

Psalm Prayer

Let us pray (pause for silent prayer):
Holy Mary, Virgin of virgins,
Mother of our Most High God:

Be our consoler and helper,
so that by your assistance
we may attain the City of God
and reign with God's chosen ones,
for ever and ever.
~Amen.

1. Reading
The Son of the Most High God
Luke 1:26–28, 30–32, 34–35

In the sixth month the angel Gabriel was sent by God to a town in Galilee called Nazareth to a virgin engaged to a man whose name was Joseph, of the house of David. The virgin's name was Mary. And he came to her and said, "Greetings, favored one! The Lord is with you. Do not be afraid, Mary, for you have found favor with God. And now, you will conceive in your womb and bear a son, and you will name him Jesus. He will be great, and will be called the Son of the Most High, and the Lord will give him the throne of his ancestor David." Mary said to the angel, "How can this be, since I am a virgin?" The angel said to her, "The Holy Spirit will come upon you, and the power of the Most High will overshadow you; therefore the child to be born of you will be holy; he will be called Son of God." Then Mary said, "Here am I, the servant of the Lord; let it be with me according to your word." Then the angel departed from her.

Pause for quiet prayer.

Responsory

The Word was made flesh, alleluia!
~The Word was made flesh, alleluia!

And lived among us, alleluia!
~The Word was made flesh, alleluia!

Glory to the Father, and to the Son,
and to the Holy Spirit:
~The Word was made flesh, alleluia!

2. A Reading of Saint Augustine of Hippo Regius on the Creed:

We believe in our Lord Jesus Christ born by the Holy Spirit of the Virgin Mary. Blessed Mary conceived in faith Him whom she bore through faith. For when a son was promised to her, she sought to learn how this could come to pass, since she knew not man. Having no experience of it herself, she knew about such matters as intercourse and birth only through what she had learned from her contact with other women; in other words, that a human being is born of the union of man and women. She received the answer from the angel: "The Holy Spirit will come upon you and the power of the Most High shall overshadow you; therefore the child to be born will be holy; he will be called Son of God" (Luke 1:35). And when the angel had said this, Mary, with complete faith, first conceived Christ in her mind before she conceived Him in her womb, as she uttered the words, "Here I am, the servant of the Lord; let it be with me according to your word" (Luke 1:38). Let a virgin conceive, she said in effect, but without the seed of man. Of the Holy Spirit and a virgin maid, let Him be born through whom the spotless Church is reborn, likewise by the Holy Spirit. Let the Holy One who is born of a human mother without a human father be called the Son of God. It was wondrously fitting that He who is born of God the Father without any mother should become the Son of Man; and that he should be born and come forth as an infant through a closed womb in that same flesh in which, after He was risen, He should as a grown-up man enter through closed doors.

St. Augustine of Hippo Regius (354–430) [25]

Pause for quiet prayer.

Responsory

Today is the beginning of our salvation, alleluia!
~TODAY IS THE BEGINNING OF OUR SALVATION, ALLELUIA!

And the revelation of the eternal mystery.
~TODAY IS THE BEGINNING OF OUR SALVATION, ALLELUIA!

Glory to the Father, and to the Son,
and to the Holy Spirit:
~TODAY IS THE BEGINNING OF OUR SALVATION, ALLELUIA!

A Litany of the Mother of God

Holy Mary, the messenger from heaven
 brought the good news to her in Nazareth of Galilee:
~Pray for us.

Holy Mary, whose divine Son came and lived
 among us for thirty years:
~Pray for us.

Holy Mary, whose anointed Son preached
 the Good News in Galilee and Judea:
~Pray for us.

Holy Mary, whose wounded Son embraced
 the cross for our sake:
~Pray for us.

Holy Mary, whose victorious Son rose
 from the grave on the third day for us:
~Pray for us.

Holy Mary, whose radiant Son ascended into heaven
 for our sake:
~Pray for us.

Holy Mary, whose blessed Son assumed you
 body and soul into heaven:
~Pray for us.

Holy Mary, whose royal Son crowned you
 Queen of all saints:
~Pray for us.

Pause for our special intentions.

Holy Mary, refuge of sinners, health of the sick,
 and consolation of the dying:
~Pray for us.

The Lord's Prayer
Lord, have mercy.
~Christ, have mercy. Lord, have mercy.
Our Father in heaven, (all in unison):

Closing Prayer
At the message of an angel
he welcomed your eternal Son
and, filled with the light of the Spirit,
Mary became the temple of your Word,
who lives and reigns with you, in the unity of the
 Holy Spirit,
one God, for ever and ever.
~Amen.

Rejoice, gracious Lady; the Lord is with you,
 alleluia!
~Blessed are you among women, alleluia!

Blessing
May the Word made flesh, full of grace and truth,
✝ bless us and keep us.
~Amen.

Mary and Eve

It is clear that Mary
is the land that receives the Source of light;
through her it has illumined
the whole world, with its inhabitants,
which had grown dark through Eve,
the source of all evils.

Mary and Eve in their symbols
resemble a body, one of whose eyes
is blind and darkened,
while the other
is clear and bright,
providing light for the whole.

Through the eye that was darkened
the whole world has darkened,
and people groped
and thought that every stone
they stumbled upon was a god,
calling falsehood truth.

By when it was illumined by the other eye,
and the heavenly Light
that resided in its midst,
humanity became reconciled once again,
realizing that what they had stumbled upon
was destroying their very life.

St. Ephrem of Edessa
(ca. 306–373)[26]

Saint Joseph of Nazareth

Joseph of Nazareth played an important role in the infancy and childhood of Jesus. As a righteous and obedient servant of the God of Israel, he accepted and supported Mary of Nazareth, his pregnant fiancée; guided her from Nazareth to Bethlehem; found a place for them to stay; arranged Jesus' circumcision and name-day ceremony; accompanied Mary to Jesus's presentation in the temple; went into exile in Egypt with Jesus and Mary; and when Jesus was twelve years old found him again in the temple. Joseph earned a living for the holy family as a workman, possibly as a carpenter. He probably died before Jesus reached manhood.

Jesus was † in the eyes of the Law, alleluia!
~THE SON OF JOSEPH, ALLELUIA!
His delight is in the law of the Lord, alleluia!
~HE MEDITATES ON IT DAY AND NIGHT, ALLELUIA!

A HYMN TO ST. JOSEPH

Joseph, we praise you, prince of God's own
    household,
Hearing the promise made of old to David,
Chosen to foster Christ, the Lord's anointed,
Son of the Father.

Strong in your silence, swift in your obedience,
Saving God's firstborn, when you fled from Herod,
Cherish God's children as you cherished Jesus,
Safe in your keeping.

Husband of Mary, one in joy and sorrow,
Share with God's people love and peace and blessing;
May your example help our homes to mirror
Nazareth's glory.

Saint of the workbench, skilled and trusted
   craftsman,
Cheerfully toiling side by side with Jesus,
Teach us to value lives of hidden splendor,
Lived in God's presence.

Husband of Mary, one in joy and sorrow,
Share with God's people love and peace and blessing;
May your example help our homes to mirror
Nazareth's glory.

Saint of the dying, when your work was ended
Jesus and Mary stood beside your deathbed;
So in life's evening may they stand beside you,
Calling us homeward.[27]

PSALM 92:1–5, 12–15 — A GOOD AND RIGHTEOUS MAN

ANTIPHON The righteous flourish like the
   palm tree, *
AND GROW LIKE A CEDAR IN LEBANON.

It is good to give thanks to the LORD,
   to sing praises to your name, O Most High;
to declare your steadfast love in the morning,
   and your faithfulness by night,
to the music of the lute and the harp,
   to the melody of the lyre.

For you, O Lord, have made me glad by your work;
  at the works of your hands I sing for joy.
How great are your works, O Lord!
  Your thoughts are very deep!

The righteous flourish like the palm tree,
  and grow like a cedar in Lebanon.
They are planted in the house of the Lord,
  they flourish in the courts of our God.

Still productive in old age,
  they are full of sap and green,
    showing that the Lord is upright.
The Lord is my rock
  in whom there is no unrighteousness.

Antiphon The righteous flourish like the palm tree,
  and grow like a cedar in Lebanon.

Psalm Prayer
Let us pray (pause for silent prayer):

God of the righteous,
you guided holy Joseph by angels
and made him the protector of the holy family
at Bethlehem, in Egypt, and at Nazareth.
By your everlasting love for us,
make him our guide and protector in this life
and especially at the hour of our death.
We ask this through Christ our Lord.
  ~Amen.

1. Reading — Jesus, Foster Son of Joseph — Luke 3:21–23

Now when all the people were baptized, and when Jesus also had been baptized and was praying, the heaven was opened, and the Holy Spirit descended upon him in bodily form like a dove. And a voice came from heaven, "You are my Son, the Beloved; with you I am well pleased." Jesus was about thirty years old when he began his work. He was the son (as was thought) of Joseph, son of Heli.

Pause for quiet prayer.

Responsory

Joseph walked blamelessly, alleluia!

~Joseph walked blamelessly, alleluia!

And spoke truth from the heart, alleluia!

~Joseph walked blamelessly, alleluia!

Glory to the Father, and to the Son,
  and to the Holy Spirit:

~Joseph walked blamelessly, alleluia!

2. A Devotional Reading on Sant Joseph by Blessed John Henry Newman

He was the true and worthy Spouse of Mary, supplying in a visible manner the place of Mary's Invisible Spouse, the Holy Spirit. He was a virgin, and his virginity was the faithful mirror of the virginity of Mary. He was the cherub, placed to guard the new terrestrial Paradise from the intrusion of every foe.

His was the father of the Son of God, because he was the spouse of Mary, ever Virgin. He was our Lord's father, because Jesus ever yielded to him the obedience of a son. He was our Lord's father, because to him was entrusted, and by him were faithfully fulfilled, the duties of a father, in protecting Him, giving Him a home, sustaining and rearing Him, and providing Him with a trade.

He is Holy Joseph, because according to the opinion of a great number of doctors, he, as well as St. John the Baptist, was sanctified even before he was born. He is Holy Joseph, because his office, of being spouse and protector of Mary, specially demanded sanctity. He is Holy Joseph, because no other saint but he lived in such and so long intimacy and familiarity with the source of all holiness, Jesus, God incarnate, and Mary, the holiest of all creatures.[28]

Pause for quiet prayer.

Responsory

Wisdom showed Joseph the kingdom of heaven, alleluia!
~WISDOM SHOWED JOSEPH THE KINGDOM OF HEAVEN, ALLELUIA!

And gave him knowledge of holy things, alleluia!
~WISDOM SHOWED JOSEPH THE KINGDOM OF HEAVEN, ALLELUIA!

Glory to the Father, and to the Son,
   and to the Holy Spirit:
~WISDOM SHOWED JOSEPH THE KINGDOM OF HEAVEN, ALLELUIA!

THE CANTICLE OF OLD SAINT SIMEON ELLC

ANTIPHON Joseph, the husband of Mary, *
   WAS THE WISE STEWARD OF THE HOLY FAMILY, ALLELUIA!

Now, Lord, † let your servant go in peace:
   your word has been fulfilled.

My own eyes have seen your salvation
   which you have prepared in the sight of every people:

a light to reveal you to the nations
   and the glory of your people Israel.

Glory to the Father, and to the Son,
   and to the Holy Spirit:
as it was in the beginning, is now,
   and will be for ever. Amen.

ANTIPHON JOSEPH, THE HUSBAND OF MARY,
   WAS THE WISE STEWARD OF THE HOLY FAMILY, ALLELUIA!

THE LORD'S PRAYER

Lord, have mercy.
~CHRIST, HAVE MERCY. LORD, HAVE MERCY.

Our Father in heaven, (all in unison):

Righteous Joseph, son of David,
~Guide your chosen people Israel.

Joseph, guardian and witness of Mary's virginity,
~Guard the chastity of all virgins.

Joseph, husband of Mary,
~Be the pillar of family life.

Joseph, guardian of the holy family,
~Help us to have the virtues of their common life.

Joseph, model of those who work with their hands,
~Make them skillful and trustworthy.

Joseph, hope of the sick and patron of the dying,
~Be with us in our final hours.

Pause for our special intentions.

Joseph, guardian of the universal Church,
~Keep and protect us, now and always.

Closing Prayer
Good Saint Joseph,
faithful guardian of the holy family,
protect the chosen people of Jesus Christ
and be our ally in our conflict
with the powers of darkness.
As you rescued the child Jesus from Herod,
defend now the universal Church from all harm.
Please listen to our prayers
and help us in all our needs.

By your help and example,
may we lead a holy life, die a godly death,
and attain to a blessed eternity in heaven.
~Amen.

Blessing
Jesus, Mary, and Joseph, I give you my heart
  and my soul.
~Amen.
Jesus, Mary, and Joseph,
  assist me in my last agony.
~Amen.
Jesus, Mary, and Joseph,
  may I breathe † forth my soul
  in peace with you.
~Amen.

Friday of the Third Week of Advent
The Visitation of Mary to Elizabeth

Impelled by the Spirit, the God-bearing Virgin hurries across the Judean hills to bring the good news to her relatives, Zachary and Elizabeth. Mary is not only the first to believe in the good news, but she is also the first human messenger of the Gospel, the first missionary, the first apostle, and the one who cares for others.

Let us celebrate † Mary's visitation to Elizabeth;
~Let us adore her Son, Christ the Lord.
God has raised up for us a mighty Savior, alleluia!
~In the house of his servant David,
  alleluia!

The Visitation

Proclaim'ed queen and mother of a God,
The light of earth, the Sovereign of Saints,
With pilgrim foot, up tiring hills she trod,
And heavenly stile with handmaid's toil acquaints;
Her youth to age, her health to sick she lends,
Her heart to God, to neighbor hand she bends.

A prince she is, and mightier prince now bears,
Yet pomp of princely train she would not have;
But doubtless heavenly quires attendant were,
Her child from harm, herself from fall to save;
Word to the voice, song to the tune she brings,
The voice her word, the tune her ditty sings.

Eternal lights enclose'ed in her breast
Shot out such piercing beams of burning love
That when her voice her cousin's ears possessed,
The force thereof did force her babe to move.
With secret signs the children greet each other,
But open praise each leaves it to his mother.

St. Robert Southwell, SJ (1561–1595),
English poet and martyr[29]

Psalm 149   The Glory of God

Antiphon The Lord has raised up for us *
A MIGHTY SAVIOR, ALLELUIA!

Sing to the Lord a new song,
   God's praise in the assembly of the faithful!
Let Israel be glad in its Maker,
   let the children of Zion rejoice in their Ruler!

Let them praise God's name with dancing,
  making melody with tambourine and lyre!
For the Lord takes pleasure in his people;
  and adorns the humble with victory.

Let the faithful exult in glory;
  let them sing for joy on their couches.
Let the high praises of God be in their throats
  and two-edged swords in their hands,

to work vengeance on the nations
  and punishment on the peoples,
to bind their rulers with fetters
  and their nobles with chains of iron,
to execute on them the judgment decreed.
  This is the glory for all God's faithful ones.

Antiphon The Lord has raised up for us a mighty Savior, alleluia!

Psalm Prayer

Let us pray (pause for quiet prayer):

Lord of the prophets,
by the birth of the holy Forerunner
enlighten the prophets and seers
of our time and place
so that the Church may praise you
and understand the needs of humanity.
We ask this through Christ our Lord.
~Amen.

The Visitation of Mary to Elizabeth

1. Reading **The Visitation** **Luke 1:39–47**

In those days Mary set out and went with haste to a Judean town in the hill country, where she entered the house of Zechariah and greeted Elizabeth. When Elizabeth heard Mary's greeting, the child leaped in her womb. And Elizabeth was filled with the Holy Spirit and exclaimed with a loud cry, "Blessed are you among women, and blessed is the fruit of your womb. And why has this happened to me that the mother of my Lord comes to me? For as soon as I heard the sound of your greeting, the child in my womb leaped for joy. And blessed is she who believed that there would be a fulfillment of what was spoken to her by the Lord." And Mary said, "My soul magnifies the Lord, and my spirit rejoices in God my Savior."

Pause for quiet prayer.

Responsory

All generations will call me blessed.

~All generations will call me blessed.

The Almighty has done great things for me.

~All generations will call me blessed.

Glory to the Father, and to the Son,
  and to the Holy Spirit.

~All generations will call me blessed.

2. A Homily of Saint John Chrysostom on John the Baptist:

Tell us, John, how you did see and hear, when you were still enclosed in the darkness of your mother's womb. How did you sense these divine things? How did you leap and exult? "A great mystery," says he, "is accomplished here, and an act far beyond human understanding. Rightly shall I do a new thing in nature because of him who will do things which are above nature. Even though I am still in the womb, I see; for I see the sun of righteousness being carried in a womb. With my ears I perceive, for I am born to be the voice of the great Word. I cry aloud, for I contemplate the only-begotten Son of the Father clothed in flesh. I rejoice, for I see the Producer of all things take the form of a man. I leap, for I think of the Redeemer of the world in the flesh. I run before his coming, and, as it were by my confession, I go before him to you."

St. John Chrysostom
(ca. 347–407)[30]

Pause for quiet prayer.

Responsory

Blessed are you among women, alleluia!
~Blessed are you among women, alleluia!

And blessed is the fruit of your womb, alleluia!
~Blessed are you among women, alleluia!

Glory to the Father, and to the Son,
  and to the Holy Spirit.
~BLESSED ARE YOU AMONG WOMEN, ALLELUIA!

THE CANTICLE OF ZEPHANIAH 3:14–20

ANTIPHON As soon as the sound of your salutation sounded in my ears, * THE CHILD IN MY WOMB LEAPED FOR JOY, ALLELUIA!

Sing aloud, O daughter Zion;
  shout, O Israel!
Rejoice and exult with all your heart,
  O daughter Jerusalem!
The LORD has taken away the judgments against
      you,
  he has turned away your enemies.
The king of Israel, the LORD, is in your midst;
  you shall fear disaster no more.
On that day it shall be said to Jerusalem:
Do not fear O Zion;
  do not let your hands grow weak.
The LORD your God is in your midst,
  a warrior who gives victory;
he will rejoice over you with gladness,
  he will renew you in his love;
he will exult over you with loud singing
  as on a day of festival.
I will remove disaster from you
  so that you will not bear reproach for it.

I will deal with all your oppressors
 at that time.
And I will save the lame
 and gather the outcast,
And I will change their shame into praise
 and renown in all the earth.
At that time I will bring you home,
 at the time that I gather you;
for I will make you renowned and praised
 among all the peoples of the earth,
when I restore all your fortunes
 before your eyes, says the LORD.

Glory to the Holy and Undivided Trinity:
 now and always and for ever and ever. Amen.

ANTIPHON AS SOON AS THE SOUND OF YOUR SALUTATION
SOUNDED IN MY EARS, THE CHILD IN MY WOMB
LEAPED FOR JOY, ALLELUIA!

A LITANY OF THE VISITATION

God of the prophets and seers, revealing your
 holy will
step by step:
~BE WITH US ALWAYS.

God of Israel, guiding and warning your chosen
 people:
~BE WITH US ALWAYS.

Lord Jesus, sanctifying John, your chosen
> forerunner,
in the womb of his mother Elizabeth:
~Be with us always.

Mary of Nazareth, carrying in your womb
the one whom the whole universe cannot
> contain:
~Be with us always.

Mary of Nazareth, singing your *Magnificat* of
> exultation
and divine promise:
~Be with us always.

Pause for our special intentions.

Commemorating our most holy, most pure, most blessed and glorious Lady, Mother of God and Ever Virgin Mary, Saint John the Baptist, and all the saints, let us commend ourselves, each other, and our whole life to Christ our God.
~To you, O Lord.

The Lord's Prayer
Lord, have mercy.
~Christ, have mercy. Lord, have mercy.

Our Father in heaven, (all in unison):

Closing Prayer
Father in heaven,
you inspired the Virgin Mary,
to visit Elizabeth and assist her in her need

and engage in holy conversation
until the birth of John the Baptist.
By the prayers of Mary and Elizabeth,
lead us into Christian friendship
and mutual service for the Kingdom of God.
We ask this through Christ our Lord.
~Amen.

BLESSING
May holy Mary and all the Saints
intercede for us with the Lord,
that we may ✝ receive help and salvation
from him who lives and reigns now and for ever.
~Amen.

Saint John the Baptist

John, a cousin of Jesus, was the last of the Old Testament prophets, the immediate forerunner of Jesus the Messiah, "'the lightgiving torch which was to precede the sun of righteousness,'"[31], the friend of the bridegroom (Mark 2:19; John 3:29). He prepared the chosen people for Christ's coming and preached repentance and the nearness of the kingdom of God. After his particular mission was accomplished, this great prophet had to die at the hands of Herod just as Jesus died at the hands of Pontius Pilate. Both preached too honestly and boldly for the princes of this world and had to suffer for it accordingly.

John's birthday (June 24) falls at the old Summer solstice just as Jesus's falls at the old Winter solstice (December 25); "He must increase and I must decrease" (John 3:30). The Baptist is the special patron of French Canada.

There was a man ✝ sent from God
~Whose name was John.
Many will rejoice at his birth,
~For he will be filled with the Holy Spirit.

Hymn

God called great prophets to foretell
The coming of his Son;
The greatest, called before his birth,
Was John, the chosen one.

John searched in solitude for Christ,
And knew him when he came;
He showed the world the Lamb of God,
And hailed him in our name.

That lonely voice cried out the truth,
Derided and denied;
As witness to the law of God
His mighty martyr died.

We praise you, Trinity in One,
The light of unknown ways,
The hope of all who search for you,
Whose love fills all our days.[32]

Psalm 146   God Is Faithful

Antiphon John was not himself the light *
but came to testify to the Light.

Praise the Lord!

Praise the LORD, O my soul!
I will praise the LORD as long as I live;
  I will sing praises to my God while I have life.

Do not put your trust in rulers,
  in mortals, in whom there is no help.
Their breath departs, they return to the earth;
  on that very day their plans perish.

Happy are those whose help is in the God of Jacob,
  whose hope is in the LORD, their God,
who made heaven and earth,
  the sea, and all that is in them;
who keeps faith for ever;
  who executes justice for the oppressed;
  who gives food to the hungry.

The LORD sets the prisoners free;
  the LORD opens the eyes of the blind.
The LORD lifts up those who are bowed down;
  the LORD loves the righteous.

The LORD watches over the aliens,
  and upholds the widow and the orphan;
but the LORD brings the way of the wicked to ruin.
  The LORD will reign for ever,
  from generation to generation.

ANTIPHON JOHN HIMSELF WAS NOT THE LIGHT BUT CAME TO TESTIFY TO THE LIGHT.

PSALM PRAYER
Let us pray (pause for quiet prayer):

Righteous God,
you raised up John the Baptist
as a fearless prophet to prepare
the way of the Lord Jesus.
May his message of repentance
dispose our minds and hearts
for the oncoming Kingdom of God
that awaits us in this world and in the next.
Blest be Jesus, the Herald of the Kingdom!
~Amen.

1. Reading   Matthew   11:11–15

Jesus said to his disciples, "Truly I tell you, among those born of women no one has arisen greater than John the Baptist; yet the least in the kingdom of heaven is greater than he. From the days of John the Baptist until now the kingdom of heaven has suffered violence, and the violent take it by force. For all the prophets and the law prophesied until John came; and if you are willing to accept it, he is Elijah who is to come. Let anyone with ears listen!"

Pause for quiet prayer.

Responsory

You shall be called the prophet of the Most High, alleluia!

~You shall be called the prophet of the Most High, alleluia!

To give God's people knowledge of salvation, alleluia!

~You shall be called the prophet of the Most High, alleluia!

Glory to the Father, and to the Son
and to the Holy Spirit:
~You shall be called the prophet of the Most High, alleluia!

2. A Reading from a Homily of Saint Ambrose, Bishop of Milan: John's Birth

Elizabeth's full time came that she should be delivered and she brought forth a son. And her neighbors rejoiced with her. The birth of a saint is a joy for many, for it is a good for all. Righteousness is a help to all, and therefore when a righteous man is born, it is a heralding of his life, which is still to come, that the helpful excellence of his future should be hailed by his neighbors. It is well that we should be told concerning the prophet, while he was yet in the womb, that we may know how that Mary was there; but we hear nothing of his childhood because that it was safe and strong through the nearness of the Lord, Himself then in that womb which was free from the pains of pregnancy. And therefore we read in the Gospel nothing touching John except his coming, the annunciation to his father and mother, the leap of joy he gave in the womb, and his crying in the wilderness.

St. Ambrose of Milan (ca. 340–397)[33]

Pause for quiet prayer.

Responsory

Elizabeth bore a son to old Zachary, alleluia!
~Elizabeth bore a son to old Zachary, alleluia!

John the Baptist, the forerunner of the Lord Christ.
~Elizabeth bore a son to old Zachary, alleluia!

Glory to the Father, and to the Son
and to the Holy Spirit:
~Elizabeth bore a son to old Zachary, alleluia!

The Canticle of Zachary   Luke 1:68–79 ELLC

Antiphon Do not be afraid, Zachary, *
your wife Elizabeth will bear you a son,
and many will rejoice at his birth, alleluia!

Blessed are you, † Lord, the God of Israel,
you have come to their people and set them free.
You have raised up for us a mighty Savior,
born of the house of your servant David.
Through your holy prophets, you promised of old
   to save us from our enemies,
   from the hands of all who hate us,
   to show mercy to our forebears,
   and to remember your holy covenant.
This was the oath you swore to our father Abraham:
   to set us free from the hands of our enemies,
   free to worship you without fear,

holy and righteous before you,
all the days of our life.

And you, child, shall be called the prophet of the
    Most High,
for you will go before the Lord to prepare the way,
to give God's people knowledge of salvation
by the forgiveness of their sins.

In the tender compassion of our God
the dawn from on high shall break upon us,
to shine on those who dwell in darkness and the
    shadow of death,
and to guide our feet into the way of peace.

Glory to the Holy and Undivided Trinity:
  now and always, and for ever and ever. Amen.

Antiphon Do not be afraid, Zachary,
  your wife Elizabeth will bear you a son,
  and many will rejoice at his birth, alleluia!

A Litany of Saint John the Baptist

In the spirit of John the Baptizer and his call
  to repentance, we pray:
~To you, O Lord.

For a full change of heart and mind, we pray:
~To you, O Lord.

For prophets to prepare us for the coming
  of our Lord in glory, we pray:
~To you, O Lord.

For preachers who are the salt of the earth
and the light of the world, we pray:
~To you, O Lord.

For the preaching and teaching of the full Gospel,
we pray:
~To you, O Lord.

Pause for our special intentions.

Commemorating our most holy, most pure, most
blessed and glorious Lady, Mother of God and
Ever Virgin Mary, with Saint John the Baptist
and his holy parents, and with all the saints, let us
commend ourselves, each other, and our whole life
to Christ our God.
~To you, O Lord.

The Lord's Prayer
Lord, have mercy.
~Christ, have mercy. Lord, have mercy.

Our Father in heaven, (all in unison):

Closing Prayer
Heavenly Father,
we enjoy the birth of John the Baptist,
the chosen forerunner of the Messiah,
who called us from our sins
and revealed to us the nearness
of the Kingdom of God.
By his merits and prayers,
may we listen carefully to his message

as his preparation for the Gospel of Jesus.
We ask this through the same Christ our Lord.
~Amen.

Blessing

May the Word made flesh, full of grace and truth,
✝ protect us and keep us.
~Amen.

III
Devotions for the Feasts of Christmastide

The thirteen devotions for the feasts of the Christmas season honor Christ the Lord from his birth to his finding in the temple at twelve years of age. Our prayers center on the two great feasts of Christmas and the Epiphany and include traditional devotions to Christ's four companions and the Solemnity of the Mother of God.

Sacred Seasons

How proper it is that Christmas should follow Advent. For those who look forward to the future, the Manger is situated on Golgotha, and the Cross has already raised in Bethlehem.

Dag Hammarskjöld (1905–1961), in *Markings*[34]

Christmas Eve

Several of the solemnities of the church have a vigil (a day before) of preparation for the feast itself. In many Catholic cultures, Christmas Eve is particularly festive in both church and home. A festive supper is often served with special foods and decorations and the blessing of the crib and the Christmas tree.

Today you will know ✝ that the Lord is coming
~AND IN THE MORNING YOU WILL SEE HIS GLORY.
Tomorrow you shall see
~THE MAJESTY OF GOD AMONG US.

PSALM 116B:12–19 RGP **JOY TO THE WORLD**

ANTIPHON How precious in the eyes of the Lord *
 IS THE DEATH OF HIS FAITHFUL.

How can I repay the LORD
for all his goodness to me?
The cup of salvation I will raise;
I will call on the name of the LORD.

My vows to the LORD I will fulfill
before all his people.
How precious in the eyes of the LORD
is the death of his faithful.

Your servant, LORD, your servant am I,
the son of your handmaid;
you have loosened my bonds.
A thanksgiving sacrifice I make;
I will call on the name of the LORD.

My vows to the LORD I will fulfill
before all his people,
in the courts of the house of the LORD,
in your midst, O Jerusalem.

ANTIPHON HOW PRECIOUS IN THE EYES OF THE LORD
 IS THE DEATH OF HIS FAITHFUL.

Psalm Prayer

Let us pray (pause for quiet prayer):

Merciful God,
you appointed your dear Son
to be the Savior of the human race
and asked Mary and Joseph
  to name him Jesus.
By this holy and awesome Name,
may we praise him in this mortal life
and enjoy the vision of him in heaven
through all eternity.
~Amen.

The Roman Proclamation of Christ's Birth:

Today, of the twenty-fifth day of December,
many ages after the creation of the world
and the formation of humanity in God's Image;
long after the flood and the primeval covenant
        with Noah;
after more than two thousand years after the
        promises
  made to our father Abraham and our mother
        Sarah;
fourteen centuries after Moses and Miriam
  and the famous exodus from the slavery of Egypt;
one thousand years after the anointing of King
        David;
in the sixty-fifth week according to the prophecy
        of Daniel;
in the one hundred and ninety-fourth Olympiad;

and the seven hundred and fifty-second year
from the founding of the City of Rome,
in the forty-second year of the reign of the Emperor
Augustus Caesar;
In the sixth age of the world, when the whole
earth was at peace,
in order to consecrate the world by his merciful
coming,
JESUS CHRIST, Son of the everlasting Father and
his Virgin
Mother Mary, was born in Bethlehem of Judea,
GOD MADE MAN.
THIS IS THE BIRTHDAY OF OUR LORD
ACCORDING
TO THE FLESH
OF OUR LORD JESUS CHRIST.[35]

A Litany of Jesus

By the will of God the name of Jesus
is highly exalted above every name:
~Thank you, Jesus.

At the name of Jesus every knee should bend
in heaven and on earth, and under the earth:
~Thank you, Jesus.

At the name of Jesus every tongue should confess
that Jesus Christ is Lord:
~Thank you, Jesus.

At the name of Jesus glory is given to God the
Father:

~THANK YOU, JESUS.

Pause for our special intentions.

At the name of Jesus, the great Mother of God,
 Mary most holy, and all the angels and saints
  falling before the throne of glory:
~THANK YOU, JESUS.

THE LORD'S PRAYER
Lord, have mercy.
~CHRIST, HAVE MERCY. LORD, HAVE MERCY.

Our Father in heaven, (all in unison):

CLOSING PRAYER
Almighty and everlasting God,
you give us with the yearly expectation
of your Son as our Redeemer,
may without fear see him coming
as our Judge;
the same Lord Jesus Christ your Son
who lives and reigns with you,
in the unity of the Holy Spirit,
one God, for ever and ever.
~AMEN.

Light dawns for the righteous, alleluia!
~AND JOY FOR THE UPRIGHT IN HEART, ALLELUIA!

BLESSING
May the Lord Jesus whose name is our salvation
✝ bless us and keep us, now and for ever.
~AMEN.

The Nativity of Christ

This is the month, and this the happy morn,
Wherein the Son of Heaven's eternal King,
Of wedded Maid and Virgin Mother born,
Our great redemption from above did bring;
For so the holy sages once did sing,
  That he our deadly forfeit should release,
And with our Father's work us a perpetual peace.

That glorious form, that light unsufferable,
And that far-beaming blaze of majesty,
Wherewith he wont at Heaven's high council-table
To sit the midst of Trinal Unity,
He laid aside; and here with us to be,
  Forsook the courts of everlasting day,
And chose with us a darksome house of mortal clay.

John Milton (1608–1674)[36]

December 25–January 1
Christmas Week

Angelic messengers convey the Good News into the darkness of this world, and heavenly light and celestial music accompany the divine message announcing the birth of the Messiah in the cave of Bethlehem. And his mother "Mary treasured all these words and pondered them in her heart" (Luke 2:10,19).

This devotion is used in the week of Christmas on December 25, 30, and 31. The Feast of the Holy Family falls on the Sunday in the octave of Christmas or on December 30, and the Solemnity of Mary on the octave day of Christmas, January 1.

The feast of Christmas was first celebrated at Rome some time before AD 336 during the reign of the Emperor Constantine. Soon it drew into its orbit the splendid mysteries of the Epiphany, the Baptism of Jesus, the Wedding Feast of Cana, and finally, the Presentation of the Lord in the Temple of Jerusalem, forty days after his birth (February 2).

After the Ecumenical Council of Ephesus (431) proclaimed Mary as *Theotokos* (Mother of God), Pope Sixtus III (432–440) restored the magnificent basilica of St. Mary Major in her honor and adorned it with splendid mosaics depicting her role in salvation history. Soon after, the pope began celebrating the main masses of Christmas in such an appropriate church.

Mary Speaks

The Son of the Most high came and dwelt in me,
and I became His mother.
Just as I gave birth to Him
   a further birth, so did He give birth to me
   a second birth: He put on His mother's robe
   her body, while I put on His glory.

St. Ephrem the Deacon (ca. 306–373)[37]

A Visit to the Cave of Bethlehem

Angels:

Whom do you seek, O Shepherds, in
   Bethlehem's cave?

Shepherds:

The Lord Christ, the Savior, as the angel said.

Question:

Who is singing in the heavens: "Glory to God
  in the highest and peace to his people on earth?"

Shepherds:

A choir of angels announcing the birth in the
  city of David, a Savior, who is the Messiah,
  the Lord.

Psalm 67:1–2:

O God be gracious to us and bless us
  and make your face shine upon us,
that your way may be known upon earth,
  your saving power among all nations.

Shepherds:

Let us go over to Bethlehem and see this thing
  that has taken place which the Lord
  has made known to us.

Let us enter the cave and find Mary and Joseph
  and the child lying in a manger between
  an ox and an ass.

Now that we have seen the holy family,
  let us tell everyone what we have heard and seen,
  and all who heard it were amazed.

Mary treasured all these words
  and pondered them in her heart.

All: Glory to the Father, and to the Son,
and to the Holy Spirit:
as it was in the beginning, is now
and will be for ever. Amen.

Prayer
Grant that we more joyfully each year
when we enter evermore into the perfect
divinity and humanity of Christ
as we set aside the old bondage of sin
and enter into perfect beauty of his light.
Through the immortality of his goodness.
~Amen.
You are † the bright and the morning Star,
~O Christ our Lord.

The Nativity of Christ
Behold the father is his daughter's son,
The bird that built the nest, is hatched therein,
The old of years an hour has not outrun,
Eternal life to live does not begin,
The Word is dumb, the mirth of heaven now
      weeps,
Might feeble is, and force does faintly creep.

O dying souls! behold your living spring!
O dazzled eyes! behold your sun of grace!
Dull ears, attend what word this word now brings!
Up heavy hearts, with joy your joy now brings!

From death, from dark, from deafness, from despair,
This life, this light, this word, this joy repairs.

Gift better than Himself God does not know,
Gift better than His God no man can see;
This gift does here the giver given bestow,
Gift to this gift let each receiver be:
God is my gift, Himself He freely gave me,
God's gift am I, and none but God shall have me.

Man altered was by sin from man to beast;
Beast's food hay is hay, hay is all mortal flesh;
Now God is flesh, and lies in manger press'ed,
As hay the brutest sinner to refresh:
O happy field wherein this fodder grew,
Whose taste does us from beasts to men renew!

St. Robert Southwell, SJ (1561–1595),
English poet and martyr[38]

PSALM 2 RGP — GOD PROCLAIMS THE ANOINTED SON

ANTIPHON You are my Son, *

TODAY I HAVE BEGOTTEN YOU, ALLELUIA!

Why do the nations conspire and the peoples plot in vain?
They arise, the kings of the earth;
princes plot against the LORD and his Anointed.
"Let us burst asunder their fetters.

Let us cast off from us their chains."

He who sits in the heavens laughs;
the Lord derides and mocks them.
Then he will speak in his anger,
his rage will strike them with terror.
"It is I who have appointed my king
on Sion, my holy mountain."

I will announce the decree of the Lord:
The Lord said to me, "You are my Son.
It is I who have begotten you this day.
Ask of me, and I will give you
the nations as your inheritance,
and the ends of the earth as your possession.
With a rod of iron you will rule them;
like a potter's jar you will shatter them."

So now, O kings, understand;
take warning, rulers of the earth.
Serve the Lord with fear;
exult with trembling, pay him your homage,
lest he be angry and you will perish on the way,
for suddenly his anger will blaze.

Blessed are all who trust in God!

Antiphon You are my Son,
today I have begotten you, alleluia!

Psalm Prayer

Let us pray (pause for quiet prayer):

Lord Jesus, Anointed Son of God,
Daystar from on high and Prince of peace,
fill the world with your splendor,
shelter us from tyrants and exploiters,
and show the nations the light of your truth.
Your reign is a reign for all ages.
~Amen.

1. Reading — **The Word of Life** — 1 John 1:1–3 TEV

Brothers and sisters, We write to you about the Word of life, which has existed from the very beginning. We have heard it, and we have seen it with our own eyes; yes, we have seen it, and our hands have touched it. When this life became visible, we saw it; so we speak of it and tell you about the eternal life which was with the Father and was made known to us. What we have seen and heard we announce to you also, so that you will join with us in the fellowship that we have with the Father and with his Son Jesus Christ.

Pause for quiet prayer.

Responsory

The Spirit of the Lord shall rest on him,
~The Spirit of the Lord shall rest on him,

The Spirit of wisdom and understanding.
~The Spirit of the Lord shall rest on him,

Glory to the Father, and to the Son,
and to the Holy Spirit:
~THE SPIRIT OF THE LORD SHALL REST ON HIM.

2. A READING FROM A HOMILY OF SAINT LEO THE GREAT († 461):

Dear Sisters and Brothers, Our Savior has been born for us today. Let us rejoice! It would not be lawful to be sad this day, for today is Life's birthday: the birthday of that life which, for us dying creatures, takes away the sting of death and brings the bright promise of everlasting life. It would be unfitting for anyone to refuse to partake in our rejoicing. Everyone has an equal share in the great cause of our joy, for our Lord, who is the destroyer of sin and death, finding that all are bound under the condemnation, is come to make all free. Rejoice, all you who are holy, for you are drawing nearer to your crown! Rejoice, you who are sinful, for your Savior offers you pardon! Rejoice also, you Gentile, for God calls you to life! For the Son of God, when the fullness of time had come, took upon the nature of man so that he might reconcile that nature to him who made it; hence the devil, the inventor of death, is met and beaten in that very flesh which had been the field of his victory.[39]

Pause for quiet prayer.

Responsory

This day Christ is born, this day the Savior has appeared.

~This day Christ is born, this day the Savior has appeared.

This day angels are singing on earth; archangels are rejoicing.

~This day Christ is born, this day the Savior has appeared.

Glory to the Father, and to the Son, and to the Holy Spirit:

~This day Christ is born, this day the Savior has appeared.

The Canticle of the Word **John 1:1–5, 10–14**

Antiphon Glory to God in the highest, alleluia! *
and peace to God's people on earth, alleluia!

In the beginning † was the Word,
 and the Word was with God,
 and the Word was God.
 He was in the beginning with God.

All things came into being through him
 and without him not one thing came into being.

What has come into being in him was life,
 and the life was the light of all people.
The light shines in the darkness,
 and the darkness did not overcome it.

He was in the world,
  and the world came into being through him;
  yet the world did not know him.
He came to what was his own,
  and his own people did not accept him.

But to all who received him,
  who believed in his name,
  he gave power to become children of God,
who were born, not of blood
  or of the will of the flesh
  or of the will of man, but of God.

And the Word became flesh
  and lived among us,
and we have seen his glory,
  the glory of the Father's only Son,
  full of grace and truth.

Antiphon Glory to God in the highest,
    alleluia!
  and peace to God's people on earth,
    alleluia!

A Christmas Litany

By the great mysteries of the Word made flesh
    for us, we pray:
~Lord, have mercy.

By the wondrous birth in time of the eternal Son
    of God, we pray:
~Lord, have mercy.

By the humble nativity of the King of glory
  in Bethlehem of Judea, we pray:
~Lord, have mercy.

By the radiant manifestation of the Babe of Bethlehem
  to the shepherds and the magi, we pray:
~Lord, have mercy.

By the meeting of the Infant Jesus with old Simeon and Anna
  in the Temple, we pray:
~Lord, have mercy.

By the lowly submission of the Maker of the world
  to Mary and Joseph of Nazareth, we pray:
~Lord, have mercy.

Pause for our special intentions.

In the communion of the great Mother of God, Mary most holy, Saint Joseph her spouse, and of all the saints in glory, let us commend ourselves, one another, and our whole life to Christ our Lord.
~To you, O Lord.

The Lord's Prayer
Lord, have mercy.
~Christ, have mercy. Lord, have mercy.

Our Father in heaven, (all in unison):

Closing Prayer

Only Begotten Son and Word of God,
immortal as you are,
You condescended
for our salvation to take flesh
from the Holy Mother of God
and Ever-Virgin Mary,
and without undergoing change,
You became Man; You were crucified,
O Christ God, and crushed death by your death;
You are One of the Holy Trinity, equal in glory
with the Father and the Holy Spirit: Save us![40]

And the Word became flesh
~AND LIVED AMONG US.

Blessing

May the Word made flesh in the Virgin's womb
✝ bless us and keep us, now and for ever.
~AMEN.

Sunday in the Octave of Christmas
The Feast of the Holy Family

Devotion to the holy family of Jesus, Mary, and Joseph grew up in Europe in the seventeenth century and spread to Canada and then throughout North America. It promotes family life on the model of the holy family. Pope Leo XIII (1810/1878–1903) fostered such a devotion, and prescribed that Christian families be dedicated to it as a remedy for the evil influences of secular and atheistic societies. Pope Bendict XV (1854/1914–1922) extended this feast to the full Roman liturgy in 1921. This feast is now observed on the Sunday in the week of Christmas or on December 30 when Christmas proper occurs on Sunday.

Our God ✝ has appeared on earth, alleluia!
~AND LIVED AMONG THE HUMAN FAMILY,
　　ALLELUIA!
Discern what is the will of God—
~WHAT IS GOOD AND ACCEPTABLE AND PERFECT.

PSALM 117 RGP　　　　　　　　　UNIVERSAL PRAISE

ANTIPHON Come, let us imitate *
　THE HOLY FAMILY OF NAZARETH.

O praise the LORD, all you nations;
acclaim him, all you peoples!
For his merciful love has prevailed over us;
and the LORD's faithfulness endures forever.

ANTIPHON COME, LET US IMITATE
　THE HOLY FAMILY OF NAZARETH.

Glory to the Father, and to the Son,
　and to the Holy Spirit:
As it was in the beginning, is now,
　and will be for ever. Amen.

ANTIPHON COME, LET US IMITATE
　THE HOLY FAMILY OF NAZARETH.

Hymn

The Light of light to darkness came,
The Word eternal to proclaim;
The Word which was before all time,
In time now dwells, the Christ divine.

Our God from all eternity,
Made flesh in our humanity,
Now cradled in a manger lies,
His kingship hidden from our eyes.

Jesus, the everlasting Word,
In you the Father's voice is heard;
In you, the Savior of our race,
We see the brightness of God's face.

True radiance of the Father's light,
Revealed in weakness to our sight,
Redeemer, prophet, priest, and King,
Your wondrous birth with joy we sing.

All praise to you, incarnate Son,
With Father and with Spirit one;
To you, O blessed Trinity,
Be praise through all eternity.[41]

Psalm 105:1–6,8–11 God's Faithful Promise

Antiphon Blessed is everyone * who walks in God's ways.

O give thanks to the Lord, call on God's name,
 make known God's deeds among the peoples!

Sing to the Lord, sing praises!
　Tell of all God's wonderful works!

Glory in God's holy name;
　let the hearts of those who seek the Lord rejoice!
Seek the Lord, the strength of the Lord;
　seek the Lord's presence continually!

Remember the wonderful works God has done,
　the miracles and judgments God has uttered,
O offspring of Abraham, God's servant,
　children of Jacob, God's chosen ones.

The Lord is mindful of the everlasting covenant,
　of the word commanded for a thousand
　　　　generations,
the covenant made with Abraham,
　the promise sworn to Isaac,
and confirmed to Jacob as a statute,
　to Israel as an everlasting covenant, saying,
"To you I will give the land of Canaan
　as your portion for an inheritance."

Antiphon Blessed is every one who
　　　　walks in God's ways.

Psalm Prayer

Let us pray (pause for silent prayer):

Faithful Lord,
your promises endure for ever
and especially in your beloved Son.
May the Holy Family model for us
the Church that stands in your sight

and enjoys your wonderful works.
Blest be Jesus, Mary, and Joseph.
~Amen.

A Reading of a Sermon of Saint Augustine of Hippo Regius:

Most worthily do all His angels praise Him who is their eternal food, who quickens their life with incorruptible sustenance; for He is the Word of God by whose life they live, by whose eternity they live forever, by whose goodness they live forever happy. Most worthily do they praise Him—God with God—and give glory to God in the highest.

"But we are His people and the sheep of His hands:" (Psalm 95:7) May we by our showing goodwill be reconciled with Him and, to the extent this is possible for our weakness, merit peace. For certainly these same words which the angels themselves uttered in their joy when the Savior was born for us, have their application today: "Glory to God in the highest, and on earth peace to those of good will" (Luke 2:14). They praise Him as they ought; let us, too, praise Him in obedience. They are His heralds; let us, on our part, be His flocks. He has filled their table in heaven; He has filled our manger on earth. For them the fullness of their table consists in this: that "in the beginning was the Word, and the Word was with God, and the Word was God" (John 1:1). For us the fullness of our manger is the fact that "the Word was made flesh, and dwelt among us"

(John 1:14). In order that we might eat the bread of
angels, the Creator of the angels was made man.
They gave praise by living, we by believing; they
by enjoying, we by asking; they by taking, we by
seeking; they by entering in, we by knocking.

St. Augustine of Hippo Regius (354–430)[42]

Pause for quiet prayer.

Responsory
Your almighty Word leapt down from heaven,
~Your almighty Word leapt down from
    heaven,
From your royal throne, O Lord.
~Your almighty Word leapt down from
    heaven,
Glory to the Father, and to the Son,
  and to the Holy Spirit:
~Your almighty Word leapt down from
    heaven.

A Christmas Litany (see page 113–14)

The Lord's Prayer
Lord, have mercy.
~Christ, have mercy. Lord, have mercy.
Our Father in heaven, (all in unison):

Closing Prayer
Lord Jesus Christ,
who was subject to Mary and Joseph

as he was virtuous and homelike,
he became more holy in every way
and always the center of the Holy Family.
He lives and reigns with God the Father,
in the unity of the Holy Spirit,
one God, for ever and ever.
~Amen.
Seek the Lord, the strength of the Lord;
~Seek the Lord's presence continually.

Blessing
To our God and Father,
to the Lord Jesus Christ,
and to the Holy and Life-giving Spirit
† be honor and glory now and for ever.
~Amen.

Comites Christi: The Companions of Christ

Devotions on the four days after Christmas honor the four "companions of Christ," witnesses and martyrs who are considered especially close to him. The first is Stephen the First Martyr, on December 26; the second, on December 27, is John the Evangelist, the primary witness of Jesus in Jerusalem; on December 28, the Holy Innocents of Bethlehem slain by Herod; and finally, on December 29, Thomas of Canterbury, slain by King Henry on December 29, 1170, on his way to Vespers. All four are considered a holy cortege to our Royal King.

December 26
Saint Stephen, the First Martyr

> Think of Stephen, called in Greek by the name "Crown," and the first to be crowned by martyrdom after the Lord's Resurrection. Think also of the many thousands who were of the number of persecutors, but who believed when the Holy Spirit came.
>
> St. Augustine of Hippo Regius (354–430)[43]

Come, † let us crown Christ the New-Born
 who crowned Stephen the Martyr.
~IN HEAVEN HE WEARS THE CROWN OF VICTORY.
I see the heavens opened, said Stephen,
~AND JESUS STANDING AT THE RIGHT HAND OF GOD.

PSALM 117 RGP   **UNIVERSAL PRAISE**

ANTIPHON Come, let us hallow Stephen, *
 FULL OF GRACE AND POWER.

O praise the LORD, all you nations;
acclaim him, all you peoples!
For his merciful love has prevailed over us;
and the LORD's faithfulness endures forever.

ANTIPHON COME, LET US HALLOW STEPHEN,
 FULL OF GRACE AND POWER.

Glory to the Father, and to the Son,
 and to the Holy Spirit:

As it was in the beginning, is now,
 and will be for ever. Amen.

ANTIPHON COME, LET US HALLOW STEPHEN, FULL OF GRACE AND POWER.

HYMN

Stephen, first of Christian martyrs,
Let the Church in hymns proclaim:
Mirroring the Savior's passion,
Thus he won immortal fame.
For his foes he prayed forgiveness
While they stoned him unto death;
To the Lord his soul commending
As he yielded up his breath.
Holy Spirit, gift of Jesus,
Shed your light upon our eyes,
That we may behold with Stephen
That fair realm beyond the skies.
Where the Son of Man in glory
Waits for us at God's right hand,
King of saints and hope of martyrs,
Lord of all the pilgrim band.
Glory be to God the Father,
Glory to his only Son,
Glory to the Holy Spirit,
Glory, endless Three in One.[44]

1. Reading   **The Death of Stephen**   **Acts 6:8–10; 7:54–60**

Now Stephen, filled with grace and power, was working great wonders and signs among the people. Certain members of the so-called Synagogue of Freedmen, Cyrenians and Alexandrians, and people from Cilicia and Asia, came forward and debated with Stephen, but they could not withstand the wisdom and the spirit with which he spoke.

When they heard this, they were infuriated, and they ground their teeth at him. But Stephen, filled with the Holy Spirit, looked up intently to heaven and saw the glory of God and Jesus standing at the right hand of God, and he said, "Behold, I see the heavens opened and the Son of Man standing at the right hand of God." But they cried out in a loud voice, covered their ears, and rushed upon him together. They threw him out of the city, and began to stone him. The witnesses laid down their cloaks at the feet of a young man named Saul. As they were stoning Stephen, he called out, "Lord Jesus, receive my spirit." Then he fell to his knees and cried out in a loud voice, "Lord, do not hold this sin against them;" and when he said this, he fell asleep.

Pause for quiet prayer.

Responsory

All who looked intently at Stephen,
~All who looked intently at Stephen,

Saw that his face was like the face of an angel.
~ALL WHO LOOKED INTENTLY AT STEPHEN,

Glory to the Father, and to the Son,
 and to the Holy Spirit:
~ALL WHO LOOKED INTENTLY AT STEPHEN.

2. A Reading from a Homily of Saint Fulgentius:

Yesterday we celebrated the birth in time of our timeless King; today we celebrate the triumphant sufferings of a soldier. Yesterday our King, clothed in a robe of flesh, came forth from a virginal womb and deigned to visit this earth; today a soldier, leaving the tabernacle of the body, departs as a conqueror for heaven. The former, preserving the majesty of divinity, assumed the lowly form of human nature and entered this world to do battle; the latter, laying aside corruptible bodily trappings, has ascended to reign unceasingly in the palaces of heaven. The one descended, veiled in flesh; the other ascended, laurelled in blood. Yesterday the angels sang: Glory to God in the highest; today they have joyously received blessed Stephen into their midst. Yesterday Christ was wrapped for us in swaddling clothes; today blessed Stephen is clothed by Him with the stole of immortality. Yesterday the narrow crib carried the Infant Christ; today the boundless heavens receive the triumphant Stephen.

Our Lord descended alone that He might make many ascend; our King has humbled Himself that He might exalt His soldiers. Nevertheless it is necessary that we know with what weapons Stephen was armed so as to overcome his Jewish enemies and merit such triumph. To obtain the crown which is signified by his name, Stephen was armed with charity and conquered all obstacles; because he prayed for those who were stoning him. In charity he corrected the erring, that they would amend; in charity he prayed for his executioners, that they would not be punished. By the virtue of charity he conquered the fire-breathing Saul and so merited to have his persecutor on earth as companion in heaven.

St. Fulgentius of Ruspe, Tunisia (468–533)[45]

Pause for quiet prayer.

Responsory

You have set on his head a crown of precious stones.
~You have set on his head a crown of precious stones.

You crowned him with honor and glory, alleluia!
~You have set on his head a crown of precious stones.

Glory to the Father, and to the Son,
and to the Holy Spirit:
~You have set on his head a crown of precious stones.

A Litany of the Martyr Stephen

Blessed Stephen, one of the first deacons
  of the early Church:
~Pray for us.

Blessed Stephen, the first of the martyrs,
  In the primitive Church:
~Pray for us.

Blessed Stephen who preached with courage
  to his fellow Jews:
~Pray for us.

Blessed Stephen, who reviewed the whole
      salvation history
  of his people:
~Pray for us.

Blessed Stephen, who saw the glory of God
  and Jesus standing at God's right hand:
~Pray for us.

Blessed Stephen, stoned to death by an irate mob:
~Pray for us.

Pause for our special intentions.

Blessed Stephen, who forgave those who stoned
      him to death:
~Pray for us.

The Lord's Prayer
Lord, have mercy.
~Christ, have mercy. Lord, have mercy.

Our Father in heaven, (all in unison):

Closing Prayer
Lord God,
we celebrate the entrance
of Stephen into eternal glory
for those who stoned him.
Help us to imitate his goodness
and to love our enemies.
We ask this through Christ our Lord.
~Amen.

Glory to God in the highest, alleluia!
~And peace to God's people on earth,
    alleluia!

Blessing
By the prayers of Saint Stephen,
may our martyred Lord
✝ bless and keep us.
~Amen.

December 27
Saint John the Evangelist

John, the Beloved Disciple, a Jerusalem Jew, was an eyewitness to the activities of Jesus. He watched the growing antagonism of the religious authorities, was present at the Last Supper, in the Garden of Gethsemane, at the trials of Jesus, and stood with Mary and the other women beneath the cross on Golgotha. During his final moments on the cross, Jesus bequeathed his mother to him, and John was present at some of the more vivid post-Resurrection scenes in

Jerusalem and on the shores of the lake of Galilee. He is often called John the Theologian or John the Divine. His Gospel is regarded as the most historical and the most theological of the four.

> The Gospel of John exercises our minds, sharpens and spiritualizes them, so that our comprehension of God is not sensual, but spiritual.
> **St. Augustine of Hippo Regius (354–430)**[46]

During the last supper, † the Beloved Disciple
~Reclined on the Lord's breast.

He is the disciple who bears witness to these things
~And we know that his witness is true.

Psalm 117 RGP   **Universal Praise**

Antiphon Come, let us hallow, *
Saint John the Evangelist and Theologian.

O praise the Lord, all you nations;
acclaim him, all you peoples!
For his merciful love has prevailed over us;
and the Lord's faithfulness endures forever.

Antiphon Come, let us hallow
Saint John the Evangelist and Theologian.

Glory to the Father, and to the Son,
and to the Holy Spirit:
As it was in the beginning, is now,
and will be for ever. Amen.

Antiphon Come, let us hallow
   Saint John the Evangelist and Theologian.

Hymn

We sing of that disciple,
Beloved of the Lord,
Who, telling all he witnessed,
Proclaimed the Father's Word;
John is that towering eagle
Who soars aloft in flight,
And with great ease discloses
The mystery of Light.

And when his hour had sounded,
John told how God revealed
The greatness of the Godhead
As Jesus quietly kneeled.
He took their feet and washed them,
As if he were their slave,
And showed the kind of kingdom
That is beyond the grave.

Then in the hour of darkness,
When he was stretched alone
Against the Tree in torment
For evil we had done,
He saw the two below him
Who stood there to the end;
And gave each to the other,
His mother and his friend.

O sing to that great eagle,
The Trumpeter of Light,
Who soars beyond the darkness
With mastery of flight.

O sing of that disciple,
Beloved of the Lord,
Whose heart had learned in Jesus
The eloquence of God.[47]

1. READING   THE WILL OF GOD   1 JOHN 1:15–17

Brothers and sisters, do not love the world or the things in the world. The love of the Father is not in those who love the world; for all that is in the world—the desire of the flesh, the desire of the eyes, the pride in riches—comes not from the Father but from the world. And the world and its desires are passing away, but those who do the will of God live for ever.

Pause for quiet prayer.

RESPONSORY

How great are your works, O Lord!
~HOW GREAT ARE YOUR WORKS, O LORD!

Your thoughts are very deep!
~HOW GREAT ARE YOUR WORKS, O LORD!

Glory to the Father, and to the Son,
  and to the Holy Spirit:
~HOW GREAT ARE YOUR WORKS, O LORD!

2. A Reading of Saint Jerome of Bethlehem:

Blessed John the Evangelist remained at Ephesus to the very last of extreme of old age. In the end, when he could scarcely endure going to church in the arms of his disciples, and when unable to speak at any length, he said nothing else than this at each gathering, "Children, love one another." Finally his disciples asked him, wearied by his repetition, "'Master, why do you say the same thing all the time?" He replied to them in a sentence worthy of John, "Because it is the Lord's command; if this is the only thing you do, it is enough!"

St. Jerome of Bethlehem (ca. 342–420)[48]

Pause for quiet prayer.

Responsory

I will satisfy him with long life, alleluia!

~I WILL SATISFY HIM WITH LONG LIFE, ALLELUIA!

And show him my salvation.

~I WILL SATISFY HIM WITH LONG LIFE, ALLELUIA!

Glory to the Father, and to the Son,
  and to the Holy Spirit:

~I WILL SATISFY HIM WITH LONG LIFE, ALLELUIA!

A Litany of Saint John the Divine

Holy John the Evangelist, who disclosed the Word made flesh:

~FILL OUR HEARTS WITH PEACE AND JOY.

Holy John the Evangelist, who was the eyewitness
of the Lord:
~Fill our hearts with peace and joy.

Holy John the Evangelist, who was the chief witness
to the divinity of Christ our Lord:
~Fill our hearts with peace and joy.

Holy John the Evangelist, the virgin disciple
whom Jesus loved:
~Fill our hearts with peace and joy.

Holy John the Evangelist, who leaned
on the Lord's breast at the last supper:
~Fill our hearts with peace and joy.

Holy John the Evangelist, who became
the guardian of the mother of Jesus
at the foot of the cross:
~Fill our hearts with peace and joy.

Holy John the Evangelist, the preacher
and teacher of love above everything:
~Fill our hearts with peace and joy.

Holy John the Evangelist, who outlived
Saint Peter the Apostle:
~Fill our hearts with peace and joy.

Holy John the Evangelist, the long-lived
disciple and witness after the death of all
the holy apostles:
~Fill our hearts with peace and joy.

Holy John the Evangelist, symbolized
   by an eagle who soars to the heights of divinity:
~FILL OUR HEARTS WITH PEACE AND JOY.

Pause for our special intentions.

Great Mother of God and John the Divine,
   pray for the Universal Church:
~FILL OUR HEARTS WITH PEACE AND JOY.

THE LORD'S PRAYER

Lord, have mercy.
~CHRIST, HAVE MERCY. LORD, HAVE MERCY.

Our Father in heaven, (all in unison):

CLOSING PRAYER

God our Father,
you have revealed the mysteries of your Word
through John, your preeminent evangelist.
By prayer and steady reflection,
may we come to understand the wisdom he taught.
We ask this through Christ our Lord.
~AMEN.

Glory to God in the highest, alleluia!
~AND PEACE TO GOD'S PEOPLE ON EARTH,
   ALLELUIA!

BLESSING

May the Word made flesh who lived among us
✝ be our Savior and our divine Lord.
~AMEN.

December 28
The Holy Innocents of Bethlehem

> Matthew's account of the death of the children of Bethlehem is stark. No attempt is made to explain or justify this horror. Rather, Matthew reminds us that Jerimiah prepared us for such a horror, warning of the loud lamentation that would come from Ramah. There Rachel would weep for her children, refusing to be consoled (Jerimiah 31:15). Rachel, moreover, rightly refuses to be consoled. The gospel—the crucifixion and resurrection of Jesus—is not a consolation for those whose children are murdered. Rather, those who follow and worship Jesus are a challenge to those who would kill children.
>
> **Stanley Hauerwas, in *Matthew*[49]**

Speechless Infants

Happy the ignorance of the infants whom Herod persecuted when he was terrified—happier than the knowledge of the men whom he consulted in his confusion! The first were able to suffer for Christ whom they had not yet been able to confess; the latter did not follow the truth of the Teacher, the city of whose birth they were able to know.

St. Augustine of Hippo Regius (354–430)[50]

Herod † is about to search for the Child
~To destroy him.
A voice was heard in Ramah,
~Wailing and loud lamentation.

Psalm 117 RGP   Universal Praise

Antiphon Come, let us hallow, *
the holy innocents of Bethlehem.

O praise the Lord, all you nations;
acclaim him, all you peoples!
For his merciful love has prevailed over us;
and the Lord's faithfulness endures forever.

Antiphon Come, let us hallow
the holy innocents of Bethlehem.

Glory to the Father, and to the Son,
 and to the Holy Spirit:
As it was in the beginning, is now,
 and will be for ever. Amen.

Antiphon Come, let us hallow
the holy innocents of Bethlehem.

Hymn

Why, Herod, so unpitying,
so fearful of the newborn king?
He seeks no mortal sovereignty,
who reigns as God eternally.

The magi traveling so far,
preceded by his natal star,

have sought with gifts, the helpless mite,
and humbly greet the Light of Light.

Now Christ, your glory is unfurled
across the nations of the world;
in humble love, revealed as Lord,
you reign, eternally adored.[51]

1. Reading   The Holy Innocents   Matthew 2:16–18

When Herod saw that he had been tricked by the wise men, he was infuriated, and sent and killed all the children in and around Bethlehem who were two years old or under, according to the time that he had learned from the wise men. Then was fulfilled what had been spoken through the prophet Jeremiah: "A voice was heard in Ramah, wailing and loud lamentation, Rachel weeping for her children; because they are no more."

Pause for quiet prayer.

Responsory

Rachel refused to be consoled;
~Rachel refused to be consoled;

Because the Innocents were no more.
~Rachel refused to be consoled;

Glory to the Father, and to the Son
 and to the Holy Spirit:
~Rachel refused to be consoled.

2. A Reading from Saint Birgitta of Sweden:

The fact that I fled into Egypt showed the weakness of my humanity and fulfilled a prophecy (Hosea 11:1). And I also gave an example to coming generations: that persecutions must be eluded for the greater glory of God in the future. Because I was not found by my pursuers, my divine plan prevailed over that of men; for it is not easy to fight against God. The fact that the infants were slain was a sign of my future passion and a mystery of election and divine charity. Although these speechless infants did not bear witness to me with their voices or their mouths, they did so through their death, as befitted my own speechless infancy; for it had been foreseen that God's praise would be accomplished even in the blood of the Innocents. . . . Where unjust malice boiled up against the children, there merit and grace justly abounded, and where confession of the tongue and age were lacking, there the blood that had been shed accumulated a most perfect goodness.

St. Birgitta of Sweden (ca. 1303–1373)[52]

Pause for quiet prayer.

Responsory

Innocent infants were slain for Christ's sake.
~**Innocent infants were slain for Christ's sake.**

The first victims for Christ our Lord.

~INNOCENT INFANTS WERE SLAIN FOR
   CHRIST'S SAKE.

Glory to the Father, and to the Son,
   and to the Holy Spirit:
~INNOCENT INFANTS WERE SLAIN FOR
   CHRIST'S SAKE.

A CHRISTMAS LITANY (SEE PAGE 113–14)

THE LORD'S PRAYER
Lord, have mercy.
~CHRIST, HAVE MERCY. LORD, HAVE MERCY.

Our Father in heaven, (all in unison):

CLOSING PRAYER
Father in heaven,
the Holy Innocents by the death
they suffered for Christ:
May our lives bear witness
to the faith we profess with our lips.
We ask this through Christ our Lord.
~AMEN.
Glory to God in the highest, alleluia!
~AND PEACE TO GOD'S PEOPLE ON EARTH,
   ALLELUIA!

BLESSING
May the children slain for Christ's sake
† pray for us to the Spotless Lamb of God.
~AMEN.

The Flight into Egypt

Alas! our Day is forced to fly by night
Light without light, and sun by silent shade
O nature blush! that suffers such a thing,
That in your Sun this dark eclipse has made;
Day to His eyes, light to His steps deny
That hates the light which graces every eye.

Sun being fled, the stars do lease their light
And shining beams in bloody streams they drench;
A cruel storm of Herod's mortal spite
Their lives and lights with bloody showers do quench:
The Tyrant to be sure of murdering one,
For fear of sparing Him do pardon none.

O blessed babes! first flowers of Christian spring,
Who though untimely cropped fair garlands frame,
With open throats and silent mouths you sing
His praise, whom age permits you not to name;
Your tunes are tears, your instruments are swords,
Your ditty death, and blood in lieu of words.

St. Robert Southwell, SJ (1561–1595),
English poet and martyr[53]

December 29
Saint Thomas of Canterbury

King Henry II of England demanded that Thomas, Archbishop of Canterbury, submit to unjust laws and customs that would make the Church subservient to the state. Thomas refused. Burning with resentment the King remarked in the hearing of his courtiers that he could no longer stand Thomas. Taking him at his word, four of his knights rode to Canterbury and slew the bishop as he was going into Vespers on December 29, 1170. Canonized in 1173, Thomas became one of the most popular of European saints. Christians created the famous pilgrimage shrine at Canterbury that became so central to English life.

Thomas of Canterbury † is a true martyr
~WHO SHED HIS BLOOD FOR CHRIST.
If any one wants to come after me,
~TAKE UP YOUR CROSS AND FOLLOW ME.

PSALM 117 RGP   **UNIVERSAL PRAISE**

ANTIPHON Come, let us hallow, *
 SAINT THOMAS OF CANTERBURY.

O praise the Lord, all you nations;
acclaim him, all you peoples!
For his merciful love has prevailed over us;
and the LORD's faithfulness endures forever.

ANTIPHON COME, LET US HALLOW
 SAINT THOMAS OF CANTERBURY.

Glory to the Father, and to the Son,
 and to the Holy Spirit:
As it was in the beginning, is now,
 and will be for ever. Amen.

ANTIPHON COME, LET US HALLOW
 SAINT THOMAS OF CANTERBURY.

Hymn

King of the martyrs' noble band,
Crown of the true in every land,
Strength of the pilgrims on their way
Beacon by night and cloud by day.

Hear us now as we celebrate
Faith undeterred by ruthless hate;
Hear and forgive us, for we too
Know very well the wrong we do.

Dying, through you they overcame;
Living, were faithful to your name.
Turn our rebellious hearts, and thus
Win a like victory in us.

Glory to God the Father be,
Glory to Christ who set us free;
And to the Spirit, living flame,
Glory unceasing we proclaim.[54]

1. Reading   The Good Shepherd   John 10:11–15

I am the good shepherd. The good shepherd lays down his life for his sheep. The hired hand, who is not the shepherd and does not own the sheep, sees the wolf coming and leaves the sheep, and runs away—and the wolf snatches them and scatters them. The hired man runs away because a hired man does not care for the sheep. I am the good shepherd. I know mine and mine know me. Just as the Father knows me and I know the Father. And I lay down my life for the sheep.

Pause for quiet prayer.

RESPONSORY

Behold a great priest who in his day pleased God.
~BEHOLD A GREAT PRIEST WHO IN HIS DAY PLEASED GOD.

I know my sheep and mine know me.
~BEHOLD A GREAT PRIEST WHO IN HIS DAY PLEASED GOD.

Glory to the Father, and to the Son,
and to the Holy Spirit:
~BEHOLD A GREAT PRIEST WHO IN HIS DAY PLEASED GOD.

2. READING FROM MURDER IN THE CATHEDRAL BY T. S. ELIOT:

THOMAS SPEAKS:

It is the just man who
Like a bold lion, should be without fear.
I am here.
No traitor to the King. I am a priest,
A Christian, saved by the blood of Christ,
Ready to suffer with my blood.
This is the sign of the Church always,
The sign of blood. Blood for blood.
His blood given to buy my life,
My blood given to pay for His death,
My death for His death.

Now to Almighty God, to the Blessed Mary ever Virgin,

To the Blessed John the Baptist, the holy
> Apostles Peter
and Paul, to the blessed martyr Denys, and to all
> the Saints,
I commend my cause and that of the Church.

> T. S. Eliot (1888–1965)[55]

Pause for quiet prayer.

Responsory

You are a priest forever in the order of
> Melchizedek.

~You are a priest for ever in the order of Melchizedek.

You are my Son, today I have begotten you,
> alleluia!

~You are a priest forever in the order of Melchizedek.

Glory to the Father, and to the Son,
and to the Holy Spirit:

~You are a priest forever in the order of Melchizedek.

Gloria in Excelsis

Glory to God in the highest,
and on earth peace to people of good will.

We praise you,
we bless you,
we adore you,
we glorify you,

we give you thanks for your great glory,
Lord God, heavenly King,
O God, almighty Father.

Lord Jesus Christ, Only Begotten Son,
Lord God, Lamb of God, Son of the Father,
you take away the sins of the world,
  have mercy on us;
you take away the sins of the world,
  receive our prayer;
you are seated at the right hand of the Father,
  have mercy on us.

For you alone are the Holy One,
you alone are the Lord,
you alone are the Most High,
Jesus Christ,
with the Holy Spirit,
in the glory of God the Father. Amen.[56]

A Christmas Litany (see page 113–14)

The Lord's Prayer
Lord, have mercy.
~Christ, have mercy. Lord, have mercy.

Our Father in heaven, (all in unison):

Closing Prayer
Almighty God,
you granted the martyr Thomas
the grace to give his life
  for the cause of justice.

By his grace
make us willing to renounce for Christ
our life in this world
so that we may find it in heaven.
We ask this through Christ our Lord.
~Amen.

Glory to God in the highest, alleluia!
~And peace to God's people on earth,
   alleluia!

Blessing
May the blessing of Thomas the Martyr
✝ strengthen the Church, now and for ever.
~Amen.

The Infant Jesus

God in the flesh of a tiny infant has always been a most beautiful devotion. He is often pictured on Mary's lap, lying on the straw of the crib in the cave of Bethlehem, being circumcised on the eighth day, receiving the Magi as they do him homage, being presented in the temple in the arms of old Simeon on the fortieth day.

Blessed be ✝ the Child of Bethlehem and Nazareth
~Who took our flesh to raise us up to his
   divine level.
The Ruler of the stars, alleluia!
~Nurses at his Mother's Breast, alleluia!

The Burning Babe

As I in hoary winter's night
  stood shivering in the snow,
Surpris'd I was with sudden heat,
  which made my heart to glow;

And lifting up a fearful eye
  to view what fire was near,
A pretty Babe all burning bright,
  did in the air appear;

Who, scorch'ed with excessive heat,
  such floods of tears did shed,
As though His floods should quench His flames,
  which with His tears were fed;

Alas! said He, but newly born,
  in fiery heats I fry,
Yet none approach to warm their hearts
  or feel my fire, but I!

My faultless breast the furnace is,
  the fuel, wounding thorns,
Love is the fire, and sighs the smoke,
  the ashes shame and scorn;

The fuel Justice lays it on
  and Mercy blows the coals,
The metal in this furnace wrought are
  men's defile'd souls;

For which, as now on fire I am,
  to work them to their good,

So will I melt into a bath
  to wash them in my blood:

With this He vanished out of sight,
  and swiftly shrunk away,
And straight I call 'ed unto mind,
  that it was Christmas Day.

> St. Robert Southwell, SJ (1561–1595),
> English poet and martyr[57]

Psalm 113 NAB God Stoops to the Humble

Antiphon God fills the hungry with good things *
AND SENDS THE RICH AWAY EMPTY, ALLELUIA!

Praise, you servants of the Lord,
  praise the name of the Lord.
Blessed be the name of the Lord
  both now and forever.
From the rising of the sun to its setting
  let the name of the Lord be praised.

High above all nations is the Lord;
  above the heavens God's glory.
Who is like the Lord,
  our God enthroned on high,
  looking down on heaven and earth?

The Lord raises the needy from the dust,
  lifts the poor from the ash heap,
seats them with princes,
  the princes of the people,
gives the childless wife a home,
  the joyful mother of children.

ANTIPHON G̱od fills the hungry with good things
and sends the rich away empty, alleluia!

Psalm Prayer

Let us pray (pause for silent prayer):
Holy Mary, holy beyond all others,
intercede with compassion for us
so that he who was born of you
and now reigns in glory
may receive our prayers
and forgive us all our sins.
We ask this in Jesus's name.
~Amen.

1. Reading   Born of a Woman   **Galatians 4:4–7 tev**

Brothers and sisters, when the right time finally came, God sent his own Son. He came as the Son of a human mother and lived under the Jewish law, to redeem those who were under the Law, so that we might become God's children. To show that you are his children, God sent the Spirit of his Son into our hearts, the Spirit who cries out, "Father, my Father." So then, you are no longer a slave but a child. And since you are his child, God will give you all that he has for his children.

Pause for quiet prayer.

The Infant Jesus

Responsory

He shall be called Emmanuel, alleluia!

~He shall be called Emmanuel, alleluia!

God-Is-with-Us, alleluia!

~He shall be called Emmanuel, alleluia!

Glory to the Father, and to the Son,
  and to the Holy Spirit.

~He shall be called Emmanuel, alleluia!

2. The Childhood of Jesus by Margaret Ebner, OP:

The childhood of our dear Lord Jesus Christ is especially close to my heart. And my devotion to it increases more and more in every way. I am granted constant, sweet, powerful grace and true loving responses by the Infant Jesus Christ. All my desires are answered by Him in this way: how with great love He descended from heaven to earth and in what littleness he entered the womb of our Lady. And He spoke, "If you placed me on a needle, you would not have been able to see me and yet I truly possessed all my members. With great delight and love I possessed her heart and with great, sweet, overflowing grace I penetrated her heart and all her members. She bore me in great joy and without difficulty." . . . I desired to hear something about His birth. Then He responded and said to me, "I was born in total purity and without pain. And my birth was as wondrous as the Holy Scriptures relate and also as the mother of Holy Christendom [the Church] believes."

Blessed Margaret Ebner, OP (1291–1351)[58]

Pause for quiet prayer.

Responsory

As a virgin she conceived, as a virgin she gave birth,

~As a virgin she conceived, as a virgin she gave birth,

A virgin she remained, alleluia!

~As a virgin she conceived, as a virgin she gave birth,

Glory to the Father, and to the Son,
and to the Holy Spirit.

~As a virgin she conceived, as a virgin she gave birth.

The Greater Doxology

Glory to God in the highest,
and on earth peace to people of good will.

We praise you,
we bless you,
we adore you,
we glorify you,
we give you thanks for your great glory,
Lord God, heavenly King,
O God, almighty Father.

Lord Jesus Christ, Only Begotten Son,
Lord God, Lamb of God, Son of the Father,
you take away the sins of the world,
   have mercy on us;

you take away the sins of the world,
  receive our prayer;
you are seated at the right hand of the Father,
  have mercy on us.

For you alone are the Holy One,
you alone are the Lord,
you alone are the Most High,
Jesus Christ,
with the Holy Spirit,
in the glory of God the Father. Amen.[59]

A Litany to the Divine Child

Lord Jesus, by your timeless generation
  from God the Father:
~Hear us, we humbly pray.

By your wonderful conception in the time
  of the Blessed Virgin Mary:
~Hear us, we humbly pray.

By your humble birth in the cave of Bethlehem:
~Hear us, we humbly pray.

By your precious name, Jesus, given
  by the angel to Mary and Joseph:
~Hear us, we humbly pray.

By your splendid manifestation to the shepherds
  of Bethlehem and the Magi from the East:
~Hear us, we humbly pray.

By your finding in the Temple after you were lost
  for three days:

~Hear us, we humbly pray.

By your loving obedience to Mary and Joseph
in the humble home of Nazareth:
~Hear us, we humbly pray.

Pause for our special intentions.

Commemorating our most holy, most pure, most blessed and glorious Lady, and Ever Virgin Mary, and with all the saints, let us commend ourselves, each other, and our whole life to Christ our God.
~To you, O Lord.

The Lord's Prayer
Lord, have mercy.
~Christ, have mercy. Lord, have mercy.

Our Father in heaven, (all in unison):

Closing Prayer
Eternal Word,
made flesh for our salvation
by the will of the eternal Father
and the consent of the Virgin Mother:
You promise to hear all those
who pray to the Father in your name.
Hear us and help us now
as you live and reign with the Father,
in the unity of the Holy Spirit,
one God, for ever and ever.
~Amen.

Blessing

May the Child of Bethlehem and Nazareth,
† bless and keep us.
~Amen.

January 1
Solemnity of the Mother of God

On January 1, the eighth day after Christmas Day, the Roman liturgy celebrates its most ancient feast of Mary, commemorating her divine maternity and perpetual virginity.

Hail, holy Mother! † The Child whom you bore
~Is the King of heaven and earth for ever.

Mary treasured all these words
~And pondered them in her heart.

Psalm 117 RGP **Universal Praise**

Antiphon Come, let us hallow *
 the great Mother of God, Mary most holy.

O praise the Lord, all you nations;
acclaim him, all you peoples!
For his merciful love has prevailed over us;
and the Lord's faithfulness endures forever.

Antiphon Come, let us hallow
 the great Mother of God, Mary most holy.

Glory to the Father, and to the Son,
 and to the Holy Spirit:

As it was in the beginning, is now,
  and will be for ever. Amen.

ANTIPHON COME, LET US HALLOW
  THE GREAT MOTHER OF GOD, MARY MOST HOLY.

To Our Blessed Lady

Sweet Queen, although thy beauty raise up me
  from sight of baser beauties here below:
  yet let me not rest there: but higher go
  to him, who took his shape from God and thee.
And if thy form in him more fair I see,
  what pleasure from his deity shall flow,
  by whose fair beams his beauty shineth so
  when I shall it behold eternally.
Then shall my love of pleasure have his fill,
  when beauty self in whom all pleasure is,
  shall my enamored soul embrace and kiss:
And shall new loves and new delights distill.
  which from my soul shall gush into my heart
  and through my body flow to every part.

Henry Constable (1562–1613)[60]

A MARIAN ANTHEM

Song of Songs 6:10; 3:6; Psalms 24:3–4; 26:6b

ANTIPHON A great sign appeared in the sky: *
  A WOMAN CLOTHED WITH THE SUN,
  WITH THE MOON UNDER HER FEET,
  AND ON HER HEAD A CROWN OF TWELVE STARS,
    ALLELUIA!

Who is this coming forth like the rising dawn,
 fair as the moon, bright as the sun,
 as beautiful as all the hosts of heaven?

~This is the great Mother of God, Mary
  most holy,
 who was conceived in grace.

Who is this coming up from the desert
 like a column of incense smoke,
breathing of myrrh and frankincense,
 and of every fine perfume?

~This is the great Mother of God, Mary
  most holy,
 who bore Christ whom nothing can
  contain.

Who is this who ascends God's holy mountain
 and stands in his sanctuary
 with clean hands and a pure heart?

~This is the great Mother of God, Mary
  most holy,
 who sits with Christ on his starry throne.

Who is this who washes her hands in innocence,
 joins the procession about the altar,
 and proclaims all God's wonders?

~This is the great Mother of God, Mary
  most holy,
 who alone, without peer,
 pleased our Lord Jesus Christ.

Who is this exalted above the choirs of angels,
 raised to the heavenly throne,
 and seated beside her divine Son in glory?

~This is the great Mother of God, Mary
 most holy,
 who intercedes for us with our Lord
 Jesus Christ.

Antiphon A great sign appeared in the sky:
 a woman clothed with the sun,
 with the moon under her feet,
 and on her head a crown of twelve stars,
 alleluia!

Prayer

Let us pray (pause for silent prayer):

Heavenly Father,
may the light of Christ's face shine upon us
to illumine our minds and hearts
to love and serve you all the days of our life.
By the merits and intercession of Mary the Virgin,
hear us and help us in all our needs
and enable us to praise you
till the ends of the earth stand in awe.
We ask this through the same Christ our Lord.
~Amen.

1. A Reading from the Holy Gospel according to Saint Luke 2:15–20:

When the angels had left them and gone into heaven, the shepherds said to one another, "Let us go now to Bethlehem and see this thing that has taken place, which the Lord has made known to us." So they went with haste and found Mary and Joseph, and the child lying in the manger. When they saw this, they made known what had been told them about this child, and all who heard it were amazed by what the shepherds told them. But Mary treasured all these words and pondered them in her heart. The shepherds returned, glorifying and praising God for all they had heard and seen, as it had been told them.

Pause for quiet prayer.

Responsory

You are more worthy of honor than the cherubim,
~You are more worthy of honor than the cherubim,

And far more glorious than the seraphim, alleluia!
~You are more worthy of honor than the cherubim,

Glory to the Father, and to the Son,
 and to the Holy Spirit:
~You are more worthy of honor than the cherubim.

2. A Reading from a Homily of Saint John Chrysostom:

Blessed Mary ever Virgin was indeed a great wonder. For what at any time has been or ever will be found more marvelous, more wonderful than she? She alone has surpassed heaven and earth in grandeur. Who more holy? No, not the Prophets, nor the Apostles, not the Martyrs, nor the Patriarchs, nor the Angels, not the Thrones, nor the Dominations, not the Cherubim, not the Seraphim nor any other living creature visible or invisible, for no one can be found greater or more excellent than Mary. At the same time she is God's handmaid and his Mother, at the same time she is a virgin and a parent. She is the Mother of Him who was begotten by the Father before every beginning, and whom the Angels and humans acknowledge as Lord of all. Do you wish to know the pre-eminence this Virgin enjoys among the heavenly hosts? Covering their faces they are present in fear and trembling, but she offers humanity to him whom she brought forth, and through her we obtain forgiveness of sins.

St. John Chrysostom (ca. 347–407)[61]

Pause for quiet prayer.

Responsory

Blessed is the great Mother of God, Mary most holy, alleluia!

~Blessed is the great Mother of God, Mary most holy,

alleluia!

She bore the Son of the eternal Father.

~Blessed is the great Mother of God, Mary most holy,

alleluia!

Glory to the Father, and to the Son
  And to the Holy Spirit:
~BLESSED IS THE GREAT MOTHER OF GOD, MARY MOST HOLY,
ALLELUIA!

THE LORD'S PRAYER

Lord, have mercy.
~CHRIST, HAVE MERCY. LORD, HAVE MERCY.

Our Father in heaven, (all in unison):

You, Christ, are the king of glory,
~THE ETERNAL SON OF THE FATHER.

When you took our flesh to set us free
~YOU HUMBLY CHOSE THE VIRGIN'S WOMB.

You overcame the sting of death
~AND OPENED THE KINGDOM OF HEAVEN TO ALL BELIEVERS.

You are seated at God's right hand in glory.
~WE BELIEVE THAT YOU WILL COME TO BE OUR JUDGE.

  Come, then, Lord, and help your people,
  ~BOUGHT WITH THE PRICE OF YOUR OWN BLOOD,

And bring us with your saints
~TO GLORY EVERLASTING.

Te Deum, Part B, ELLC [62]

Pause for our special intentions.

Closing Prayer

God our Father,
may we always profit by the prayers
of the Virgin Mother Mary,
for you bring us life and salvation
through Jesus Christ her Son,
who lives and reigns with you,
in the unity of the Holy Spirit,
one God, for ever and ever.
~Amen.

Glory to God in the highest, alleluia!
~And peace to God's people on earth,
    alleluia!

Blessing

May the unceasing prayers of the Virgin Mary
✝ bring down upon us every blessing.
~Amen.

Antiphon for the Virgin

Pierced by the light of God
Mary Virgin,
drenched in the speech of God,
your body blossomed,
swelling with the breath of God.

For the Spirit purged you
of the poison Eve took.
She soiled all freshness when she caught

that infection
from the devil's suggestion.

But in wonder within you
you hid an untainted
child of God's mind
and God's Son blossomed in your body.

The Holy One was his midwife:
his birth broke the laws
of flesh that Eve made. He was coupled
to wholeness
in the seedbed of holiness.

St. Hildegard of Bingen (1098–1179)[63]

January 5
The Vigil of the Epiphany

Just as Christmas enjoys a vigil so does the Solemnity of the Epiphany. In the United States and Canada the Solemnity of the Epiphany is celebrated on the first Sunday after January 1 and the Feast of the Baptism of the Lord on the second Sunday. However, in private usage we may use the ancient dates in January.

The Lord is ✝ coming, O Jerusalem,
~AND THE GLORY OF THE LORD WILL SHINE
   UPON YOU.
The star points out the king of Israel
~AND THE MAGI OFFER GIFTS TO THE LORD OF ALL.

Hymn

What star is this, with beams so bright,
More lovely than the noon-day light,
'Tis sent to announce a new born king,
Glad tidings to our God to bring.

'Tis now fulfilled what God decreed,
"From Jacob shall a star proceed";
And lo! The Eastern sages stand,
To read in heav'n the Lord's command.

O Jesus, while the star of grace
Impels us on to seek your face,
Let not our slothful hearts refuse
The guidance of your light to use.

To God the Father, heavenly Light,
To Christ, revealed in earthly night,
To God the Spirit now we raise
An endless song of thankful praise!

Charles Coffin, 1736; revised John Chandler, 1837[64]

Psalm 96:1–3,7–13 RGP

All Creation Praises God

Antiphon The Lord our Savior *
WILL APPEAR TO-MORROW, ALLELUIA!

O sing a new song to the LORD;
sing to the LORD, all the earth.
O sing to the LORD; bless his name.
Proclaim God's salvation from day to day.

Tell among the nations his glory,
and his wonders among all the peoples.

Give the Lord, you families of peoples,
give the Lord glory and power;
give the Lord the glory of his name.

Bring an offering and enter his courts;
worship the Lord in holy splendor.
O tremble before him, all the earth.

Say to the nations, "The Lord is king."
The world he made firm in its place;
he will judge the peoples in firmness.

Let the heavens rejoice and earth be glad;
let the sea and all within it thunder praise.
Let the land and all it hears rejoice.

Then shall all the trees of the wood shout for joy
at the presence of the Lord, for he comes.

Antiphon The Lord our Savior
will appear to-morrow, alleluia!

Psalm Prayer

Let us pray (pause for quiet prayer):

Lord God of Israel,
who raised a new star in the heavens
to reveal the new born King:
May we follow in the steps of the Magi
and offer Jesus the homage he deserves.
His reign is a reign for all ages.
~Amen.

1. Reading   Genuine Love   Romans 12:9–13

Brothers and sisters, let love be genuine; hate what is evil, hold fast to what is good; love one another with mutual affection; outdo one another in showing honor. Do not lag in zeal, be ardent in spirit, serve the Lord. Rejoice in hope, be patient in suffering, persevere in prayer. Contribute to the needs of the saints; extend hospitality to strangers.

Pause for quiet prayer.

Responsory

Everyone who believes that Jesus is the Christ is
> born of God.
~Everyone who believes that Jesus is the
> Christ is born of God.

For the Spirit is the truth, alleluia!
~Everyone who believes that Jesus is the
> Christ is born of God.

Glory to the Father, and to the Son,
and to the Holy Spirit.
~Everyone who believes that Jesus is the
> Christ is born of God.

2. The Star in the Heavens

What a great and wonderful mystery! We must recognize the kind of Mediator we have between God and humanity: From the very beginning of his birth, he united the divine and the human, the lowest with the highest. Jesus was born of a woman but a woman who remained a virgin; wrapped in swaddling clothes but honored by angelic praise; hidden in a crib but revealed by a star in the heavens.

St. Bernard of Claivaux(1090–1153)[65]

Pause for quiet prayer.

Responsory

A holy day dawns upon us, alleluia!
~A holy day dawns upon us, alleluia!

Come, you nations and adore the Lord, alleluia!
~A holy day dawns upon us, alleluia!

Glory to the Father, and to the Son,
 and to the Holy Spirit.
~A holy day dawns upon us, alleluia!

Gloria in Excelsis

Glory to God in the highest,
and on earth peace to people of good will.

We praise you,
we bless you,
we adore you,
we glorify you,
we give you thanks for your great glory,
Lord God, heavenly King,
O God, almighty Father.

Lord Jesus Christ, Only Begotten Son,
Lord God, Lamb of God, Son of the Father,

you take away the sins of the world,
   have mercy on us;
you take away the sins of the world,
   receive our prayer;
you are seated at the right hand of the Father,
   have mercy on us.

For you alone are the Holy One,
you alone are the Lord,
you alone are the Most High,
Jesus Christ,
with the Holy Spirit,
in the glory of God the Father. Amen.[66]

The Lord's Prayer

Lord, have mercy.
~Christ, have mercy. Lord, have mercy.

Our Father in heaven, (all in unison):

Closing Prayer

All-powerful Father,
you sent your Son Jesus Christ
to bring the new light of salvation to the world.
May he enlighten us with his radiance,
who lives and reigns with You,
In the unity of the Holy Spirit,
one God, for ever and ever.
~Amen.

Worship the Lord in holy splendor;
~Tremble before the Lord, all the earth!

BLESSING
May the divine assistance
† remain always with us.
~AMEN.

The Epiphany

The Epiphany celebrates the revelation of God the Son as a human being in Jesus Christ. Western Christians typically celebrate the visit of the Magi to the infant Jesus—Christ's manifestation to the gentiles. The Eastern Church emphasizes the baptism of Jesus—the revelation of Jesus as the Son of God. In the United States and Canada the Solemnity of the Epiphany is celebrated on the first Sunday after January 1 and the Feast of the Baptism of the Lord on the second Sunday.

A DEVOTION OF THE MAGI TO THE CHRIST CHILD

Mary was the first to welcome the Messiah and his messianic gifts by faith. Joseph unhesitatingly embraced God's puzzling ways in pure faith. A handful of shepherds, enveloped in light and celestial music, went and saw the child in the cradle. And now, a few Magi, following a star, became the first-fruits of the gentiles to believe. Even before Paul the apostle, this last sign gave way to the coming of the universal Church. Both the shepherds of Bethlehem and the wise men from afar knew, "Arise, shine; for your light has come, and the glory of the Lord has risen upon you" (Isaiah 60:1).

The Gifts of the Magi

Jesus said, "With great love and with strong faith the three kings sought me. They found me with great joy and brought me worthy gifts both inwardly and outwardly." . . . After that I asked my Salvation, Jesus, what happened to the great gifts that have been given to you, since you remained so poor? The Child said, "The lowest good does not belong to the Highest Good. I did not descend from heaven in order to enjoy earthly riches. My mother gave them to the poor.'"

Blessed Margaret Ebner, OP (1291–1351)[67]

A Visit by the Magi to Bethlehem

Question: Whom do you seek, O wise men, from the East?

Answer: The new-born King of the Jews.

Question: Who indicated this king to you?

Answer: We observed his star at its rising and have come
to pay him homage.

Question: Why is King Herod so frightened and all Jerusalem
with him?

Answer: Because the priests told him that the Messiah
was born in Bethlehem of Judea.

Psalm 117: Praise the Lord, all you nations!
Give glory, all you peoples!
The Lord's love for us is strong;
the Lord is faithful for ever!

Question: How did you find the Messiah on Mary's lap?
Answer: By the leading of the star that we had seen at its rising
until it stopped over the place where the child was
and were overwhelmed with joy.
Question: What gifts did you give him as you paid him homage?
Answer: We offered him gifts of gold, frankincense, and myrrh:
Gold for a king, incense for a God, and myrrh for a burial.
All: Glory to the Father, and to the Son, and to the Holy Spirit:
as it was in the beginning, is now
and will be for ever. Amen.

Prayer

Lord God,
who on this day by the leading of a star
you showed your only Son to the Gentiles:
Graciously grant that we who know by faith
may be brought to the beauty of your majesty.
In Jesus's name we ask it.
~Amen.

We saw ✝ his star at its rising, alleluia!
~**And have come to do him homage, alleluia!**

The Epiphany

To blaze the rising of this glorious sun
A glittering star appears now in the East.
Whose sight to pilgrim-toils three sages won
To seek the light they long had in request;
And by this star to nobler star they pass,
Whose arms did their desired Sun embrace.

Stall was the sky wherein these planets shined,
And want the cloud that did eclipse their rays;
Yet through this cloud their light did passage find,
And pierced these sages' hearts by secret ways,
Which made them know the Ruler of the skies,
By infant tongue and looks of babish eyes.

Heaven at her light, earth blushes at her pride,
And of their pomp these peers ashamed be;
their crowns, their robes, their train they set aside,
When God's poor cottage rags, and crew they see;
And glorious things their glory now despise,
Since God's contempt, does more then glory prize.

Three gifts they bring, three gifts they bear away;
For incense, myrrh, and gold—faith, hope, and love;
And with their gifts the givers' hearts do stay,
Their mind from Christ no parting can remove;
His humble state, his stall, his poor retinue
They fancy more, than all their rich revenue.

St. Robert Southwell, SJ (1561–1595),
English poet and martyr[68]

A Canticle of Isaiah the Prophet

60:1–3, 11, 14

ANTIPHON Nations shall come to your light, *
AND KINGS TO THE BRIGHTNESS OF YOUR DAWN.

Arise, shine; for your light has come,
and the glory of the LORD has risen upon you.
For darkness shall cover the earth,
and thick darkness the peoples;
but the LORD will arise upon you,
and his glory will appear over you.

Your gates shall always be open;
day and night they shall not be shut,
so that the nations shall bring you their wealth,
with their kings led in procession.

The descendants of those who oppressed you
shall come bending low to you,
and all who despised you
shall bow down at your feet;
they shall call you the City of the LORD,
the Zion of the Holy One of Israel.

ANTIPHON NATIONS SHALL COME TO YOUR LIGHT,
AND KINGS TO THE BRIGHTNESS OF YOUR DAWN.

PRAYER

Let us pray (pause for silent prayer):

Lord Jesus, light of the world,
shine on those who sit in darkness
and the shadow of death

and bring all the nations
into your glorious and everlasting light;
for your reign is a reign for all ages.
~Amen.

1. Reading — **The Coming of the Magi** — **Matthew 2:1–11**

In the time of King Herod, after Jesus was born in Bethlehem of Judea, wise men from the East came to Jerusalem, asking, "Where is the child who has been born king of the Jews? For we observed his star at its rising, and have come to pay him homage." When King Herod heard this, he was frightened, and all Jerusalem with him; and calling together the chief priests and all the scribes of the people, he inquired of them where the Messiah was to be born. They told him, "In Bethlehem of Judea; for so it has been written by the prophet:

'And you, Bethlehem, in the land of Judah,
 are by no means least among the rulers
   of Judah;
for from you shall come a ruler
 who is to shepherd my people Israel.'"

Then Herod secretly called for the wise men and learned from them the exact time when the star had appeared. Then he sent them to Bethlehem, saying, "Go and search diligently for the child; and when you have found him, bring me word so that I may also go and pay him homage." When they had heard the king, they set out; ahead of them, went the star that they had seen at its rising, until it stopped over the place where the child was. When they saw that the star had stopped, they were overwhelmed with joy. On entering the house they saw the child with Mary his mother; and they knelt down and paid him homage. Then, opening their treasure chests, they offered him gifts of gold, frankincense, and myrrh.

Pause for quiet prayer.

Responsory

The magi knelt down and paid him homage,
> alleluia!

~The magi knelt down and paid him homage, alleluia!

They offered him mystical gifts of gold,
> frankincense, and myrrh.

~The magi knelt down and paid him homage, alleluia!

Glory to the Father, and to the Son,
> and to the Holy Spirit.

~The magi knelt down and paid him homage, alleluia!

2. A Reading of a Sermon of Saint Augustine of Hippo Regius:

A few days ago we celebrated the Lord's Nativity; today we are celebrating Epiphany—a Greek word meaning "manifestation," and referring to what the Apostle says: "Without doubt, great is the mystery

of godliness which was manifested in the flesh."
(1 Timothy 3:16). Accordingly, both days pertain
to Christ's manifestation. In fact, on the first He
was born a human being of His human mother, He
who without beginning was God with the Father.
But He was manifested in the flesh to the flesh;
because the flesh was not able to see Him as He was
in the spirit. And it was also on that day, which is
called his birthday, that the Jewish shepherds saw
Him; whereas on this day, which is properly called
"Manifestation," the Gentile Magi adored Him.
Angels announced Him to the former, but a star to
the latter. The heavens are inhabited by the angels
and are adorned by the stars; to both, then, did "the
heavens show forth the glory of God" (Psalm 19:2).

St. Augustine of Hippo Regius (354–430)[69]

Pause for quiet prayer.

Responsory

The Magi were seeking for finding, alleluia!
~The Magi were seeking for finding,
  alleluia!

Herod's search was for the purpose of destruction.
~The Magi were seeking for finding,
  alleluia!

Glory to the Father, and to the Son,
  and to the Holy Spirit.
~The Magi were seeking for finding,
  alleluia!

A Litany of the Epiphany

By the sacred mysteries of the Word made flesh,
we pray:
~Christ, have mercy.

By his wondrous birth in time of the timeless Son
of God, we pray:
~Christ, have mercy.

By the humble nativity of the King of glory in
Bethlehem's cave, we pray:
~Christ, have mercy.

By the splendid manifestation of the King of the Jews
to the shepherds and the Magi, we pray:
~Christ, have mercy.

By the meeting with old Simeon and Anna
when Jesus first visited the Temple, we pray:
~Christ, have mercy.

By the flight of the holy family into Egypt
and their years of exile there, we pray:
~Christ, have mercy.

By the loss and finding of Jesus in the Temple
when he was twelve years old, we pray:
~Christ, have mercy.

For the conversion of the whole human race
to the Savior of the world, we pray.
~Christ, have mercy.

Pause for our special intentions.

In communion with the great Mother of God,
Mary most holy, Saint John the Baptist, good
Saint Joseph, and all the company of saints, let us
commend ourselves, one another, and our whole
life to Christ our Lord:
~To you, O Lord.

The Lord's Prayer
Lord, have mercy.
~Christ, have mercy. Lord, have mercy.

Our Father in heaven, (all in unison):

Closing Prayer
Lord God of the nations,
you chose servants to reveal your mysteries:
From among the angel choirs, Gabriel;
from all human beings, the Virgin Mary;
from the heavenly host, the star of Bethlehem;
from the seas and rivers, the Jordan,
to wash away the sins of the whole world.
Glory to you, O Lord, glory to you!
~Amen.

A wondrous mystery is revealed today;
~Natures are renewed, God has
    become man.

Doxology
To our God and Father,
to the Lord Jesus Christ,

and to the Holy and Life-giving Spirit
✝ be honor and glory, now and for ever.
~Amen.

The Presentation of Jesus in the Temple

As was required by the Mosaic Law, Mary and Joseph presented heir first-born in the temple at Jerusalem forty days after his birth. Another God-fearing couple, old Simeon and Anna, joyously welcome the Lord of the temple, the light of the nations and the glory of Israel, and, at the same time, predict the ominous course of his life and that of his mother Mary.

Historically, the Presentation might have occurred after the coming of the Magi. Liturgically, however, in the Roman and Byzantine liturgies, this feast is observed on February 2.

The Temple

The prophetic theme of this first coming of Jesus to the Temple is already the same as that of the second, when he comes to purify [and replace] the Temple. The first feature of the new reality Christ brings is the universal scope of salvation; God's house will be open to all nations. This universal significance of the Presentation completes the earlier meaning of the hidden coming of Christmas Day, when the angels and people of every condition acclaimed or acknowledged the Lord.

Yves Congar, OP (1904–1995)[70]

In the name of the Father, † and of the Son,
and of the Holy Spirit.
~A<small>MEN</small>.

Joseph and Mary took the Child to Jerusalem
~<small>TO PRESENT HIM TO THE LORD, ALLELUIA!</small>

P<small>SALM</small> 117 <small>RGP</small>　　　　　　　　**A<small>N</small> I<small>NVITATION TO</small> P<small>RAISE</small> O<small>UR</small> G<small>OD</small>**

A<small>NTIPHON</small>　Come, let us adore Christ *
<small>WHO REVEALED HIMSELF TO JEW AND
GENTILE ALIKE,
ALLELUIA!</small>

O praise the Lord, all you nations;
acclaim him, all you peoples!
For his merciful love has prevailed over us;
and the Lord's faithfulness endures forever.

A<small>NTIPHON</small>　C<small>OME, LET US ADORE</small> C<small>HRIST
WHO REVEALED HIMSELF TO</small> J<small>EW AND</small> G<small>ENTILE
ALIKE,
ALLELUIA!</small>

Glory to the Father, and to the Son,
and to the Holy Spirit:
as it was in the beginning, is now,
and will be for ever. Amen.

A<small>NTIPHON</small>　C<small>OME, LET US ADORE</small> C<small>HRIST
WHO REVEALED HIMSELF TO</small> J<small>EW AND</small> G<small>ENTILE
ALIKE,
ALLELUIA!</small>

The Presentation

To be redeemed the world's Redeemer brought,
Two simple turtle doves for ransom pay;
O! goods with empires worthy to be bought,
This easy rate now sounds not drowns your praise!
For since no price can to your worth amount,
A dove, yes love, due price you do account.

Old Simeon, for bargain cheap and sweet
Obtained, when you in arms he did embrace;
His weeping eyes your smiling looks did meet,
Your love his heart, your kisses blessed his face:
O eyes! O heart! mean sights and loves avoid,
Base not your selves, your best you have enjoyed.

O Virgin pure! you did these doves present
As due to law, not as an equal price;
To buy such goods you would your life have spent;
The world to reach his worth could not suffice;
If God were to be bought, not worldly wealth,
But you, were best price next to God Himself.

St. Robert Southwell, SJ (1561–1595),
English poet and martyr[71]

1. Reading   **Old Simeon**   **Luke 2:22, 25–28, 33–35**

When the time came for their purification according to the law of Moses, they brought him up to Jerusalem to present him to the Lord. Now there was a man in Jerusalem whose name was Simeon; this man was righteous and devout, looking forward to the consolation of Israel, and the Holy Spirit rested upon him. It had been revealed to him by the Holy Spirit that he would not see death before he had seen the Lord's Messiah. Guided by the Spirit, Simeon came into the temple; and when the parents brought in the child Jesus, to do for him what was customary under the law, Simeon took him in his arms and praised God. The child's father and mother were amazed at what was being said about him. Then Simeon blessed them and said to his mother Mary, "This child is destined for the falling and rising of many in Israel, and to be a sign that will be opposed so that the inner thoughts of many will be revealed—and a sword will pierce your own soul too."

Pause for quiet prayer.

Responsory

The child's father and mother were amazed, alleluia!
~The child's father and mother were
 amazed, alleluia!

At what was being said about him, alleluia!
~The child's father and mother were
 amazed, alleluia!

Glory to the Father, and to the Son,
 and to the Holy Spirit.
~The child's father and mother were
 amazed, alleluia!

Or this reading:

2. Reading   Anna the Prophet   Luke 2:36–38

There was also a prophet, Anna, the daughter of Phanuel, of the tribe of Asher. She was of great age, having lived with her husband seven years after her marriage, then as widow to the age of eighty-four. She never left the temple but worshiped there with fasting and prayer night and day. At that moment she came, and began to praise God and to speak about the child to all who were looking for the redemption of Jerusalem.

Pause for quiet prayer.

Responsory

You are a light of revelation to the Gentiles.
~You are a light of revelation to the Gentiles.

And for glory to your people Israel.
~You are a light of revelation to the Gentiles.

Glory to the Father, and to the Son,
 and to the Holy Spirit.
~You are a light of revelation to the Gentiles.

Or this reading:

3. A Reading of Saint Augustine of Hippo Regius:

Just now when the Gospel was read, we heard that Simeon, a most saintly old man, received a divine revelation that he would not taste "death before he has seen the Christ of the Lord" (Luke 2:26). And when he had taken the infant Christ in his hands and recognized the Child for His greatness, he said: "Now, Lord, let your servant go in peace: your word has been fulfilled. My own eyes have seen your salvation" (Luke 2:29). Let us, then, with eloquent tongue "tell His salvation from day to day" (Psalm 96:2). Let us "declare His glory among the nations, his marvelous works among all the peoples" (Psalm 96:3).

St. Augustine of Hippo Regius (354–430)[72]

Pause for quiet prayer.

Responsory

The Virgin Mary presented the Child Jesus in the Temple.
~The Virgin Mary presented the Child Jesus in the Temple.

Old Simeon took Him in his arms and blessed God for ever, alleluia!
~The Virgin Mary presented the Child Jesus in the Temple.

Glory to the Father, and to the Son, and to the Holy Spirit.
~The Virgin Mary presented the Child Jesus in the Temple.

THE CANTICLE OF OLD SIMEON LUKE 2:29–32ELLC

ANTIPHON Zion adorn your bridal chamber *
AND WELCOME CHRIST YOUR KING.
GREET MARY WITH OPEN ARMS,
FOR SHE IT IS WHO BRINGS US HEAVEN ITSELF,
ALLELUIA! [73]

Now, Lord, you let your servant go in peace:
your word has been fulfilled.

My own eyes have seen the salvation
which you have prepared in the sight of every
 people.
a light to reveal you to the nations
and the glory of your people Israel.

Glory to the Holy and Undivided Trinity:
now and always and for ever and ever. Amen.

ANTIPHON ZION ADORN YOUR BRIDAL CHAMBER
AND WELCOME CHRIST YOUR KING.
GREET MARY WITH OPEN ARMS,
FOR SHE IT IS WHO BRINGS US HEAVEN ITSELF,
ALLELUIA!

A LITANY OF THE PRESENTATION

Great God and Savior Jesus Christ, show yourself
 to all the ends of the earth:
~HEAR OUR PRAYERS, O LORD.

Reveal yourself to the house of Israel
 and to all the nations of the world:
~HEAR OUR PRAYERS, O LORD.

184 Devotions for the Feasts of Christmastide

Show yourself to all who await your coming:
~Hear our prayers, O Lord.

Reveal yourself to the poor and wretched of the earth:
~Hear our prayers, O Lord.

Show yourself to the sick and the dying:
~Hear our prayers, O Lord.

Reveal yourself to those most in need of you:
~Hear our prayers, O Lord.

Pause for our special intentions.

By the prayers of the Virgin Mary
  and of all the saints, show yourself
  to a waiting world:
~Hear our prayers, O Lord.

The Lord's Prayer
Lord, have mercy.
~Christ, have mercy. Lord, have mercy.

Our Father in heaven, (all in unison):

Closing Prayer
Lord Jesus Christ,
you appeared among us in human likeness,
and were presented in the temple
  by your parents,
where old Simeon and Anna welcomed
  and blessed you.

Grant that we, too,
may truly know and faithfully love you,
now in this present life
and through all the ages of ages.
~Amen.

Declare his glory among the nations,
~His marvelous works among all the
   peoples.

Blessing

May Christ, Son of Mary and Son of God,
† bless us and keep us.
~Amen.

Christ's Return Out of Egypt

At the time of the coming of the Messiah, the chosen people of God were ruled by a pagan emperor and by a client king of Rome, Herod the Great (37 BC–AD 4), at best half-Jewish, a master of politics, and wild and ungovernable in his personal life. Thanks to his loyalty to Augustus Caesar he was able to expand his kingdom from Judea to include Idumea, Samaria, Galilee, Perea, and the ancient and fertile Bashan in the northeast of Palestine.

He was a dangerous ruler to his own family and to anyone who threatened his throne. His murderous instincts revealed themselves in his slaughter of the Holy Innocents of Bethlehem, a ferocious attempt to kill off the new-born Messiah. His successor, Herod Agrippa I, was almost as dangerous, and the holy family fled to Egypt to escape his wrath. This devotion celebrates the holy family's return from Egypt.

Your glory is chanted † above the heavens;
~BY THE MOUTH OF BABES AND INFANTS.

May all who seek you, alleluia!
~REJOICE AND BE GLAD IN YOU, ALLELUIA!

Christ's Return from Egypt

When death and hell their right in Herod claim,
Christ from exile returns to native soil,
There, with His life more deeply death to maim,
Then death did life by all the infants spoil.
He showed the parents that their babes did moan,
That all their lives were less than His alone.

But hearing Herod's son to have the crown,
An impious offspring of a bloody sire,
To Nazareth (of heaven belov'ed) town,
Flower to a flower, he fitly does retire;
For lover He is and in a flower he bred,
And from a thorn now to a flower he fled.

And well deserved this flower His fruit to view,
Where he invested was in mortal need;
Where first unto a tender bud He grew,
In virgin branch unstained with mortal seed:
Young flower with flowers in flower may he be,
Ripe fruit he must with thorns hang on a tree.

St. Robert Southwell, SJ (1561–1595),
English poet and martyr[74]

The Canticle of Judith   16:13–16

Antiphon O Lord, there is none *
THAT CAN RESIST YOUR VOICE.

I will sing to my God a new song:
  O Lord, you are great and glorious,
  wonderful in strength, invincible.

Let all your creatures serve you,
  for you spoke, and they were made.
You sent forth your spirit, and it formed them.
  there is none that can resist your voice.

For the mountains shall be shaken
  to their foundations with the waters;
  before your glance the rocks shall melt like wax.
But to those who fear you show mercy.

For every sacrifice as a fragrant offering is a
      small thing,
  and the fat of all burnt offerings to you is a
      little thing:
but whoever fears the Lord is great forever.

Glory to the Holy and Undivided Trinity:
  now and always and for ever and ever. Amen.

Antiphon O Lord, there is none
THAT CAN RESIST YOUR VOICE.

Psalm Prayer

Let us pray (pause for silent prayer):

Holy God and Father of us all,

who rescued the holy family from the rage of Herod
and restored them to their humble home
in the little town of Nazareth of Galilee.
As we stand in your holy presence,
permit us to offer you the worship you deserve
in union with the Virgin Mother of God,
the good Saint Joseph,
and the whole company of heaven;
through the merits of Jesus Christ our Lord.
~Amen.

1. Reading   The Death of Herod   Matthew 2:19–23

When Herod died, an angel of the Lord appeared in a dream to Joseph in Egypt and said, "Get up, take the child and his mother, and go to the Land of Israel, for those who were seeking the child's life are dead." Then Joseph got up, took the child and his mother, and went to the land of Israel. But when he heard that Archelaus was ruling over Judea in place of his father, he was afraid that he was there. And after being warned in a dream, he went away to the district of Galilee. There he made his home in a town called Nazareth, so that what had been spoken through the prophets might be fulfilled, "He will be called a Nazorean."

Pause for quiet prayer.

Responsory

When Joseph awoke from sleep, alleluia!
~**When Joseph awoke from sleep, alleluia!**

He did as the Angel commanded him.
~**When Joseph awoke from sleep, alleluia!**

Glory to the Father, and to the Son,
 and to the Holy Spirit:
~**When Joseph awoke from sleep, alleluia!**

2. Reading   Tyrants Die

The good news is that Herod dies. Crafty as he was, his craftiness could not save him from death. Kings come and go, but God's people endure, because God has made endurance possible through the kingdom begun in Jesus. So again, while in Egypt, an angel appears and tells Joseph of Herod's death, stating that he should return to Israel. Joseph never hesitates. With Mary and Jesus, Joseph returns, but the return is not without danger. Archelaus, Herod's son, now rules Judea (Matthew 2:23).

Stanley Hauerwas, in *Matthew* [75]

Pause for quiet prayer.

Responsory

This is my Son, the Beloved, alleluia!
~**This is my Son, the Beloved, alleluia!**

With whom I am well pleased.
~**This is my Son, the Beloved, alleluia!**

Glory to the Father, and to the Son,
  and to the Holy Spirit:
~**This is my Son, the Beloved, alleluia!**

Gloria in Excelsis

Glory to God in the highest,
and on earth peace to people of good will.

We praise you,
we bless you,
we adore you,
we glorify you,
we give you thanks for your great glory,
Lord God, heavenly King,
O God, almighty Father.

Lord Jesus Christ, Only Begotten Son,
Lord God, Lamb of God, Son of the Father,
you take away the sins of the world,
  have mercy on us;
you take away the sins of the world,
  receive our prayer;
you are seated at the right hand of the Father,
  have mercy on us.

For you alone are the Holy One,
you alone are the Lord,
you alone are the Most High,
Jesus Christ,
with the Holy Spirit,
in the glory of God the Father. Amen.[76]

A Litany of the Epiphanies

By the sacred mysteries of the Word made flesh,
> we pray:

~Christ, have mercy.

By his wondrous birth in time of the timeless Son
> of God, we pray:

~Christ, have mercy.

By the humble nativity of the King of glory
> in Bethlehem's cave, we pray:

~Christ, have mercy.

By the splendid manifestation of the King of
> the Jews
to the shepherds and the Magi, we pray:

~Christ, have mercy.

By the meeting with old Simeon and Anna
when Jesus first visited the Temple, we pray:

~Christ, have mercy.

By the flight of the holy family into Egypt
and their years of exile there, we pray:

~Christ, have mercy.

By the loss and finding of Jesus in the Temple
when he was twelve years old, we pray:

~Christ, have mercy.

Pause for our special intentions.

Commemorating our most holy, most pure, most
blessed and glorious Lady, Mother of God and

Ever Virgin Mary, and with all the saints, let us commend ourselves, each other, and our whole life to Christ our God.
~To you, O Lord.

THE LORD'S PRAYER
Lord, have mercy.
~Christ, have mercy. Lord, have mercy.

Our Father in heaven, (all in unison):

CLOSING PRAYER
Lord God of Israel,
protector of the holy family
as they fled to exile in Egypt
and returned in safety to Nazareth:
Be the guardian of your holy Church,
save it from the tyrants of our age,
and deliver us from the evil one,
now and for ever.
~Amen.

BLESSING
O God, be gracious to us † and bless us,
and make your face shine upon us,
and let all the peoples praise you!
~Amen.

Jesus at Twelve Years of Age

Two important periods of silence and obscurity prevailed in Jesus's life: from his birth in Bethlehem until after the coming of the Magi; the later one after he was found by his parents in the Temple where he spoke for the first time in the Gospel. Apparently the first period was for several years, but there is no way of finding out. The second period lasted for eighteen years until his baptism in the Jordan and the beginning of his public life.

This devotion to Jesus at twelve years of age ends our cycle of devotions celebrating the coming of Christ among us.

Bless † the Lord, O my soul!
~O Lord, my God, you are very great!
You are clothed with honor and majesty,
~And wrapped in light as with a garment!

Psalm 117 rgp **An Invitation to Praise Our God**

Antiphon Come, let us adore Jesus *
 at Twelve Years of Age.

O praise the Lord, all you nations;
acclaim him, all you peoples!
For his merciful love has prevailed over us;
and the Lord's faithfulness endures forever.

Antiphon Come, let us adore Jesus
 at Twelve Years of Age.

Glory to the Father, and to the Son,
 and to the Holy Spirit:

as it was in the beginning, is now,
   and will be for ever. Amen.

ANTIPHON C**OME, LET US ADORE** J**ESUS**
   AT T**WELVE** Y**EARS OF** A**GE**.

Christ's Childhood

Till twelve years' age, how Christ His
      childhood spent,
All earthly pens unworthy were to write;
Such acts to mortal eyes he did present,
Whose worth not men but angels must recite:
No nature's blots, no childish faults defiled,
Where Grace was guide and God did play the child.

In springing ringlets lay concealed an ancient wit,
In semblance young, a grave and ancient bearing;
In lowly looks high majesty did sit,
In tender tongue sound sense of sagest sort:
Nature imparted all that she could teach,
And God supplied where Nature could not reach.

His mirth, of modest mean a mirror was,
His sadness tempered with a mild aspect;
His eye to try each action was a glass,
Whose looks did good approve and bad correct;
His natures' gifts, His grace, His word and deed,
Well showed that all did from a God proceed.

> St. Robert Southwell, SJ (1561–1595),
> English poet and martyr[77]

READING   **LOSS AND FIND**   **LUKE 2:41–50**

Now every year his parents went to Jerusalem for the festival of the Passover. And when he was twelve years old, they went up as usual for the festival. When the festival had ended and they started to return, the boy Jesus stayed behind in Jerusalem, but his parents did not know it. Assuming that he was in the group of travelers, they went a day's journey. Then they started to look for him among their relatives and friends. When they did not find him, they returned to Jerusalem to search for him. After three days they found him in the temple, listening and asking them questions. And all who heard him were amazed at his understanding and his answers. When his parents saw him they were astonished; and his mother said to him, "Child, why have you treated us like this? Look, your father and I have been searching for you in great anxiety." He said to them. "Why were you searching for me? Did you not know that I must be in my Father's house? But they did not understand what he said to them.

Pause for quiet prayer.

RESPONSORY

"Why were you looking for me," said Jesus.
~"WHY WERE YOU LOOKING FOR ME," SAID JESUS.

"Did you not know that I must be at my Father's?"
~"WHY WERE YOU LOOKING FOR ME," SAID JESUS.

Glory to the Father, and to the Son,
  and to the Holy Spirit:
~"WHY WERE YOU LOOKING FOR ME," SAID JESUS.

THE LORD'S PRAYER

Lord, have mercy.
~CHRIST, HAVE MERCY. LORD, HAVE MERCY.

Our Father in heaven, (all in unison):

You, Christ, are the king of glory,
~THE ETERNAL SON OF THE FATHER.

When you took our flesh to set us free
~YOU HUMBLY CHOSE THE VIRGIN'S WOMB.

You overcame the sting of death
~AND OPENED THE KINGDOM OF HEAVEN TO ALL BELIEVERS.

You are seated at God's right hand in glory.
~WE BELIEVE THAT YOU WILL COME TO BE OUR JUDGE.

Come, then, Lord, and help your people,
~BOUGHT WITH THE PRICE OF YOUR OWN BLOOD,

and bring us with your saints
~TO GLORY EVERLASTING.

Te Deum, Part B, ELLC[78]

CLOSING PRAYER

Please grant us, O Lord,
that we may be always joyful,
in health of soul and body.

By the prayers of the glorious Virgin Mary
may be delivered from our sorrows
that now afflict us and be joyful instead;
by our Lord Jesus Christ, your Son,
who lives and reigns with you,
in the unity of the Holy Spirit,
one God, for ever and ever.
~Amen.[79]

Holy and wondrous is God's name!
~**The praise of the Lord endures forever.**

Blessing
May Mary the Virgin of virgins
and her Joseph her virgin husband
✝ intercede for us with the Lord.
~Amen.

IV Prayers for Christmas and Advent

The Daily Angelus

This daily devotion was begun by the Franciscans in the thirteenth century to pray for peace in the turbulent states and cities of Italy and to commemorate the incarnation of Christ with the cooperation of Mary, his mother and ours. Traditionally it is said three times a day—at 6 AM, noon, and 6 PM. The Angelus is a particularly fitting devotion during Advent and Christmastide.

The Annunciation

God brought our blessed Lady to my understanding. I saw her with my understanding as though she were with me physically: a simple maid and meek, so young she seemed like a mere child—yet the very same age when she conceived. And God showed me then something of the wisdom and truth of her soul. In particular, I saw her attitude toward God her Maker, how she marveled with great reverence when he wished to be born of her, who was a mere and simple creature he himself had made. It was this wisdom, this truth, seeing how great was her Maker compared to her own littleness, that made her say to Gabriel, "Behold me, God's handmaid." Then I knew for certain that she was more worthy and more full of grace than all the rest of God's creation, with the sole exception of the manhood of Christ.

                Blessed Julian of Norwich (ca. 1342–1416)[80]

The angel of the Lord brought the good news
> to Mary,

~AND SHE CONCEIVED BY THE HOLY SPIRIT.

Hail, Mary, full of grace, the Lord is with you.
Blessed are you among women,
and blessed is the fruit of your womb, JESUS.

~HOLY MARY, MOTHER OF GOD, PRAY FOR US
> SINNERS,

NOW, AND AT THE HOUR OF OUR DEATH. AMEN.

I am the Lord's servant;
~LET IT HAPPEN AS THE LORD WILLS.

Hail, Mary, full of grace, the Lord is with you.
Blessed are you among women,
and blessed is the fruit of your womb, JESUS.

~HOLY MARY, MOTHER OF GOD, PRAY FOR US
> SINNERS,

NOW, AND AT THE HOUR OF OUR DEATH. AMEN.

The Word was made flesh,
~AND DWELT AMONG US.

Hail, Mary, full of grace, the Lord is with you.
Blessed are you among women,
and blessed is the fruit of your womb, JESUS.

~HOLY MARY, MOTHER OF GOD, PRAY FOR US SINNERS,
  NOW, AND AT THE HOUR OF OUR DEATH. AMEN.

Pray for us, holy Mother of God,
~THAT WE MAY BECOME WORTHY OF THE
    PROMISES OF CHRIST.

Let us pray:

Pour forth, O Lord, your grace into our hearts,
that we, to whom the incarnation of Christ
      your Son
was made known by the message of an angel,
may by his passion and cross
be brought to the glory of his resurrection.
We ask this through the same Christ our Lord.
~AMEN.

To Our Lady Mother

O Mother-Maid, O Maiden-Mother free!
O bush unburned, burning in Moses' sight,
That ravished down from heaven the Deity
Whose Spirit, drawn so humbly, did alight,
Kindling within your womb the Holy Light,

Conceived there as the Father's Sapience,
Help me to tell it in your reverence!

Lady, your bounty, your magnificence,
Your virtue and your great humility
No tongue can tell, expressed in sound or sense,
For sometimes, Lady, even before we see
The need, you go ahead, of your benignity,
To bring us, by your prayer, the Light so clear,
That guides our footsteps to your Son so dear.

My skill so weak is, blissful Queen,
To tell in verse your own great worthiness
That I may not the weight of it sustain,
But as a child of twelve months old or less,
Who scarcely can the smallest word express
Thus do I come, and therefore you I pray:
Guide now my song that I of you shall say.

Geoffrey Chaucer (ca. 1343–1400)[81]

The Coming

And God held in his hand
A small globe. Look, he said.
The son looked. Far off,
As through water, he saw
A scorched land of fierce
Colour. The light burned
There; crusted buildings
Cast there shadows; a bright
Serpent, a river

Uncoiled itself, radiant
With slime.

On a bare
Hill a bare tree saddened
The sky. Many people
Held out their thin arms
To it, as though waiting
For a vanished April
To return to its crossed
Boughs. The son watched
Them. Let me go there, he said.

R. S. Thomas (1913–2000)[82]

Mary and Eve

It is clear that Mary
is the land that receives the Source of light;
through her it has illumined
the whole world, with its inhabitants,
which had grown dark through Eve,
the source of all evils.

Mary and Eve in their symbols
resemble a body, one of whose eyes
is blind and darkened,
while the other
is clear and bright,
providing light for the whole.

Through the eye that was darkened
the whole world has darkened,

and people groped
and thought that every stone
they stumbled upon was a god,
calling falsehood truth.

By when it was illumined by the other eye,
and the heavenly Light
that resided in its midst,
humanity became reconciled once again,
realizing that what they had stumbled upon
was destroying their very life.

St. Ephrem of Edessa (ca. 306–373)[83]

Saint Francis of Assisi and Christmas at Greccio

84. What Francis did on the birthday of our Lord Jesus Christ near the little town called Greccio in the third year before his glorious death . . . In that place there was a certain man by the name of John, of good reputation and an even better life, whom blessed Francis loved with a special love. . . . Blessed Francis sent for this man about fifteen days before the birth of the Lord and said to him, "to celebrate the feast of the Lord at Greccio, go with haste and diligently prepare what I tell you. For I wish to do something that will recall to memory the little Child who was born in Bethlehem set before our bodily eyes and in some ways the inconveniences of his infant needs,

how he lay in a manger, how, with an ox and an ass standing by, he lay upon the hay where he had been placed." When the good and faithful man heard these things, he ran with haste and prepared in that place all the things the saint had told him.

85. But the day of joy drew near, the time of great rejoicing came. The brothers were called from their various places. Men and women of that neighborhood prepared with glad heart, according to their means, candles and torches to light up that night that has lighted up all the days and years with its gleaming star. At length the saint of God came, and finding all things prepared, he saw it and was glad. The manger was prepared, the hay has been brought, the ox and the ass were brought in. There simplicity was honored, poverty was exalted, humility was commended, and Greccio was made, as it were, a new Bethlehem. The night was lighted up like the day, and it delighted men and beasts. The people came and were delighted with new joy over the new mystery. The woods rang with the voices of the crowd and the rocks made answer to their jubilation. The brothers sang, paying their debt of praise to the Lord, and the whole night resounded with their rejoicing. The saint of God stood before the manger, uttering sighs, overcome with love, and filled with wonderful happiness. The solemnities of the Mass

were celebrated over the manger and the priest experienced a new consolation.

86. The saint of God was clothed with the vestments of the deacon, and he sang the holy Gospel in a sonorous voice. There he preached to the people standing about, and he spoke charming words concerning the nativity of the poor King and the little town of Bethlehem"

Thomas of Celano, OFM (1185–1260)[84]

A Prayer to the Child Jesus

O Lord Jesus,
who became a child for love of us,
we still contemplate you in Bethlehem,
and we place around you and around Mary,
your Mother and ours,
around Joseph that just man,
and around the good, simple shepherds,
these young hopes of our Christian families,
who have come from all over the world.
Every one of these offers,
for our joy and encouragement,
melodious singing, a pure heart,
and the fervent and heartfelt intention
to do honor to Holy Church
and to the fine traditions of the people
of various continents so brilliantly represented here.
Bless them, O Jesus, as we bless them in your name.

Be with them along the road, so rich in promise,
that opens before them.
May they bring joy and beauty wherever they go.
Following your example, may they grow in years,
In grace, in wisdom, in the sight of God and
        all humans.
Amen.[85]

Before the Paling of the Stars

Before the paling of the stars,
  Before the winter morn,
Before the earliest cock crow
  Jesus Christ was born:
  Born in a stable,
  Cradled in a manger,
In the world His hands had made
  Born a stranger.

Priest and king lay fast asleep
  In Jerusalem,
Young and old lay fast asleep
  In crowded Bethlehem:
Saint and angel, ox and ass,
  Kept a watch together,
Before the Christmas daybreak
  In the winter weather.

Jesus on His mother's breast
  In the stable cold,
Spotless Lamb of God was He,
  Shepherd of the fold:

Let us kneel with Mary maid,
  With Joseph bent and hoary,
With saint and angel, ox and ass,
  To hail the King of Glory.

Christina Rossetti (1830–1894)[86]

To St. John the Baptist

Of course you are the messenger, you who
  Shed the grey brightness which the sun
      breaks through.
As when pale dawn provokes the birds to play
  Their music glorifies the shape of day,
So your birth violates your father's tongue
  Till, from his lips, a shriek of praise is wrung.
And as the sun burns red when the last gleam
  Of styptic dawn admits a blood-red stream,
Your blood, too, gushes on the world whose fate
  The sun you herald will illuminate.

Andrzej Morsztyn (Poland ca. 1613–1693)[87]

The Nativity of Christ

This is the month, and this the happy morn,
Wherein the Son of Heaven's eternal King,
Of wedded Maid and Virgin Mother born,
Our great redemption from above did bring;
For so the holy sages once did sing,
  That he our deadly forfeit should release,
And with our Father's work us a perpetual peace.

That glorious form, that light unsufferable,
And that far-beaming blaze of majesty,
Wherewith he wont at Heaven's high council-table
To sit the midst of Trinal Unity,
He laid aside; and here with us to be,
　Forsook the courts of everlasting day,
And chose with us a darksome house of mortal clay.

John Milton (1608–1674)[88]

The One Mediator

The art of mercy unites the beatitude of God and the misery of man in one Mediator. By virtue of the Incarnation and the Resurrection, beatitude absorbs misery and life swallows up death. The whole man is glorified and passes over into union with the divine nature. Divine honor has assumed without guilt all the infirmities that human nature is subject to with guilt. Divinity did not refuse the weakness of infancy or wish to share beginnings other than those of the common lot. There was one exception. Born immaculate of an immaculate mother through the Holy Spirit he cleansed the blemishes of our origin and instituted for us the sacrament of second birth.

The Christmas Sermons of Blessed Guerric of Igny[89]

In Excelsis Gloria

When Christ was born of Mary free,
In Bethlehem in that fair city,
Angels sung e'er with mirth and glee,
　　In excelsis gloria!

Herdsmen beheld these angels bright
To them appeared with great light,
And said, "God's Son is born this night:"
　　In excelsis gloria!

This King is come to save his kind,
In the scripture as we find;
Therefore this song have we in mind:
　　In excelsis gloria!

Then, dear Lord, for thy great grace,
Grant us in bliss to see they face,
Where we may sing to thy solace.
　　In excelsis gloria![90]

A Christmas Devotion

This private devotion issued from the piety of the Capuchin Franciscan order and is used during the Christmas season and at other times during the year.

1. Lord Jesus,
    you proceeded from the heart
    of the eternal Father
    for our salvation
    and were conceived

by the power of the Holy Spirit
in the womb of the Virgin Mother.

~WORD MADE FLESH, HAVE MERCY ON US.

2. Lord Jesus,
by the visit of your Mother Mary
to her cousin Elizabeth,
John the Baptist, your herald and forerunner,
was filled with the Holy Spirit,
and danced for joy in his mother's womb.

~WORD MADE FLESH, HAVE MERCY ON US.

3. Lord Jesus,
though he was in the form of God,
did not regard equality with God,
as something to be exploited,
but humbled himself,
and enclosed himself for nine months
in Mary's womb.

~WORD MADE FLESH, HAVE MERCY ON US.

4. Lord Jesus,
you were born in Bethlehem of Judea,
wrapped in swaddling clothes,
and laid in a manger;
you were heralded by angel choirs,
and discovered by wondering shepherds.

~WORD MADE FLESH, HAVE MERCY ON US.

> Blest Author of this earthly frame
> To take a servant's form he came,
> That liberating flesh by flesh

Whom he had made might live afresh.
Christ stands near us, alleluia!

~COME, LET US ADORE HIM, ALLELUIA!

5. Lord Jesus,
on the eighth day after your birth,
you were circumcised
and given the name Jesus,
the name revealed to both Joseph and Mary
before your conception.

~WORD MADE FLESH, HAVE MERCY ON US.

6. Lord Jesus,
by the leading of a star,
the Gentile Magi found you in Bethlehem,
adored you on Mary's lap,
and honored you with mystical gifts
of gold, frankincense, and myrrh.

~WORD MADE FLESH, HAVE MERCY ON US.

7. Lord Jesus,
forty days after your birth,
your parents presented you in the Temple,
old Simeon received you in his arms,
and the aged Anna spoke of you to all
who were looking for the redemption of
    Jerusalem.

~WORD MADE FLESH, HAVE MERCY ON US.

8. Lord Jesus,
after the visit of the Magi,

an angel appeared to Joseph in a dream
and commanded him to escape into Egypt
with you and your Mother.

~WORD MADE FLESH, HAVE MERCY ON US.

    All glory, Jesus, be to you,
for evermore the Virgin's Son,
to Father and to Paraclete
be praises while endless ages run!
Christ was born for us, alleluia!

~COME, LET US ADORE HIM, ALLELUIA!

9. Lord Jesus,
your flight into Egypt snatched you
from cruel Herod's hands,
but a voice was heard in Ramah,
wailing and loud lamentation,
Rachel weeping for her children,
because they were no more.

~WORD MADE FLESH, HAVE MERCY ON US.

10. Lord Jesus,
after cruel Herod's death,
an angel again appeared to Joseph
and recalled you home to Galilee,
and to the little town of Nazareth.

~WORD MADE FLESH, HAVE MERCY ON US.

11. Lord Jesus,
in the humble home of Nazareth,
you lived obediently to your parents,
were known as the carpenter's son,

and grew in wisdom and age,
and in divine and human favor.

~Word made flesh, have mercy on us.

12. Lord Jesus,
when you were twelve years old,
after Passover you lingered in Jerusalem,
and dismayed your parents by your loss
until they found you in the Temple,
sitting among the teachers,
listening to them and asking them questions.

~Word made flesh, have mercy on us.

> Mary, Mother whom we bless,
> full of grace and tenderness,
> defend me from the devil's power
> and greet me in my dying hour. Amen.
> The Word was made flesh, alleluia!

~And lived among us, alleluia!

Let us pray:

Our Father in heaven,
you reveal yourself to the little ones
and invite them into your Kingdom.
As we recall with devotion
the mysteries of your Son's childhood
and try to walk in his footsteps,
may we attain the Kingdom of Heaven
he promised to those who receive it
as if they were little children.

We ask this through Christ our Lord.
~Amen.[91]

Carol

Flocks feed by darkness with a noise of whispers,
In the dry grass of pastures,
And lull the solemn night with their weak bells.

The little towns on the rocky hills
Look down as meek as children:
Because they have seen come this holy time.

God's glory, now, is kindled gentler than
    low candlelight
Under the rafters of a barn:
Eternal Peace is sleeping in the hay,
And Wisdom born in secret in a
    straw-roofed stable.

And O! Make holy music in the stars, you
    happy angels,
You shepherds gather on the hill.
Look up, you timid flocks, where the tree kings
Are coming through the wintry trees;

While we unnumbered children of the
    wicked centuries
Come after with our penances and our prayers,
And lay them down in the sweet-smelling hay
Beside the wise men's golden jars.

Thomas Merton (1915–1968)[92]

The Virgin Mary

Oh Virgin Mother, daughter of your Son,
  most humble, most exalted of all creatures
  chosen of God in His eternal plan,

you are the one who ennobled human nature
  to the extent that He did not distain,
  Who was its Maker, to make Himself man.

Within your womb rekindled was the love
  that gave the warmth that did allow this flower
  to come to bloom within this timeless peace.

For all up here you are the noonday torch
  of charity, and down to earth, for men,
  the living spring of their eternal hope.

Lady, you are so great, so powerful,
  that who seeks grace without recourse to you
  would have his wish fly upward without wings.

Not only does your loving kindness rush
  to those who ask for it, but often times
  it flows spontaneously before the plea.

In you is tenderness, in you is pity,
  in you munificence—in you unites
  all that is good in God's created beings.

Dante Alighieri (1265–1321)[93]

Tota pulchra es, Maria

Tota pulchra es, Maria,
et macula non est in te.

Tu gloria Jerusalem,
Tu laetitia Israel,
tu honorificentia populi nostri.
Tu advocata peccatorum,
O Maria, Virgo prudentissima,
Mater clementissima,
ora pro nobis
ad Dominum Jesum Christum.

You are altogether beautiful, Mary,
and there is no flaw in you.
You are the glory of Jerusalem,
you are the greatest boast of Israel,
you are the great pride of our nation.
Queen conceived in grace,
Queen raised up to glory,
Refuge of sinners, health of the sick,
pray for us to our Lord Jesus Christ.[94]

Antiphon for the Virgin

Pierced by the light of God
Mary Virgin,
drenched in the speech of God,
your body blossomed,
swelling with the breath of God.

For the Spirit purged you
of the poison Eve took.
She soiled all freshness when she caught
that infection
from the devil's suggestion.

But in wonder within you
you hid an untainted
child of God's mind
and God's Son blossomed in your body.

The Holy One was his midwife:
his birth broke the laws
of flesh that Eve made. He was coupled
to wholeness
in the seedbed of holiness.

Saint Hildegard of Bingen (1098–1179)[95]

Christmas Eve Prayers

THE BLESSING OF THE CRIB IN THE HOME
The crib (crèche, cradle, or manger) is best put on the family altar or on a low table near the Christmas tree. In our Catholic traditions it is best to erect both the tree and the crib during the last days of the fourth week of Advent and keep them up until the close of the Christmas season on February 2.

Sing a well-known carol.

Read from the Holy Gospel of St. Luke 2:1–20.

BLESSING OF THE CRIB WITH HOLY WATER

Blessing
Jesus of Bethlehem,
you came down from heaven
to teach us that we are children of God.
Please † bless this crib

that reminds us of your birth
in the cave of the City of David;
and teach us to love you with all our hearts
and be kind to all our neighbors.
By the affectionate prayers of Mary and Joseph,
keep us safe and sound, now and for ever.
~Amen.

The Blessing of the Tree
The tree reminds us of the tree of Paradise and all its fruits and flowers that result from the saving gifts of Jesus. Like the Advent wreath the tree and the crib are sacramentals that declare the good news of Christ.

Read from the prophet Isaiah 9:6–7.

A Christmas Tree Prayer
God our Father,
every year we rejoice in the feast of Christmas
and all its promises.
May we welcome Jesus into our home
and meet him with trust and hope
when we meet Him at the end of time.
We ask this through Christ our Lord.
~Amen.

The Flight into Egypt

Alas! our Day is forced to fly by night
Light without light, and sun by silent shade
O nature blush! that suffers such a thing,
That in your Sun this dark eclipse has made;

Day to His eyes, light to His steps deny
That hates the light which graces every eye.

Sun being fled, the stars do lease their light
And shining beams in bloody streams
      they drench;
A cruel storm of Herod's mortal spite
Their lives and lights with bloody showers do
      quench:
The Tyrant to be sure of murdering one,
For fear of sparing Him do pardon none.

O blessed babes! first flowers of Christian spring,
Who though untimely cropped fair
      garlands frame,
With open throats and silent mouths you sing
His praise, whom age permits you not to name;
Your tunes are tears, your instruments are swords,
Your ditty death, and blood in lieu of words.

St. Robert Southwell, SJ (1561–1595),
English poet and martyr[96]

Notes

1. The Athanasian Creed. This text is taken from the *Roman Breviary in English*, Volume 1 (New York: Benziger Brothers, Inc., 1950), 52–54.
2. Saint Leo the Great (✝ 461), a Homily on the Lord's Ascension, translated by William G. Storey.
3. Saint Augustine of Hippo Regius (354–430), *Sermon 13 de Tempore*, translated by William G. Storey.
4. Charles Wesley (1707–1788), *Hymns for the Nativity of the Lord* (London: William Strahan, 1745).
5. The O Antiphons of the Roman Liturgy of Advent, translated by William G. Storey.
6. Christina Rossetti (1830–1894), "Love Came Down at Christmas," 1885.
7. Leonardo Boff, OFM, *The Maternal Face of God* (San Francisco: Harper & Row, 1987), 130.
8. Saint Robert Southwell, SJ (1561–1595), *Collected Poems of St. Robert Southwell*, edited by Peter Davidson and Anne Sweeney (Manchester, UK: Carcanet Press Ltd., 2007).

Author's note: These poems were created by the heroic and learned Jesuit missionary to the persecuted and suppressed Catholics of England during the reign of Elizabeth Tudor (1533/1558–1603). After six years of ministering to the Catholic underground, he was finally betrayed and captured in 1592, imprisoned in the Tower of London, and frightfully tortured ten times over two and a half years, kept in a filthy hole, tried for treason, and hanged, drawn, and quartered at Tyburn in 1595.

In order to facilitate the praying of these poems, I have noted a few archaic words and provided reasonable provisions for modern users. I would also suggest that these poems be read carefully several times before praying them. After that exercise, continuing to pray them will reveal their depth of religious meaning and sensibility.

9. *Lumen Gentium,* Vatican Council II, November 21, 1964, Chapter VII, "Our Lady," edited by Austin Flannery, OP (New York: Costello, 1996), 82–83.

10. Hymn at the Vespers of December 8, in *The Winter Pascha,* Thomas Hopko (Crestwood, NY: St. Vladimir's Seminary Press, 1997), 43–44.

11. A Byzantine Troparion, in *Byzantine Daily Worship,* Joseph Raya and Jose de Vinck (Allendale, NJ: Alleluia Press, 1969), 438.

12. Saint Robert Southwell, SJ (1560–1595), *Collected Poems of St. Robert Southwell,* edited by Peter Davidson and Anne Sweeney (Manchester, UK: Carcanet Press Ltd., 2007).

13. Saint Augustine of Hippo Regius (354–430), a homily of Saint Augustine in *A Short Breviary* (Collegeville, MN: Liturgical Press, 1949), 662–663.

14. *Byzantine Daily Worship,* November 21, Joseph Raya and Jose de Vinck (Allendale, NJ: Alleluia Press, 1969), 515, 518.

15. Stanbrook Abbey Hymnal © 1974 and 1995.

16. The Proto-Gospel of James, in *The Apocryphal Gospels: Texts and Translations,* Bart D. Ehrman and Zlatko Plese (New York: Oxford University Press, 2011), 49.

17. John Keble (1792–1866) and William John Hall (1793–1861).

18. Golden Legend of James de Varagine, OP (ca. 1230–1298).

19. Stanbrook Abbey Hymnal © 1974 and 1995.

20. *Nican Mopohua,* #22–23, in *Guadalupe: Mother of the New Creation,* translated by Virgil Elizondo (Maryknoll, NY: Orbis Books, 1998), 7–8.

21. Saint Robert Southwell, SJ (1561–1595), *Collected Poems of St. Robert Southwell,* edited by Peter Davidson and Anne Sweeney (Manchester, UK: Carcanet Press Ltd., 2007).

22. Saint John of Damascus (ca. 675–ca. 749), Homily I on the Dormition of the Holy Mother of God, in *On the Dormition of Mary: Early Patristic Homilies*, translated by Brian E. Daley, SJ (Crestwood, NY: St. Vladimir's Seminary Press, 1997), 189.

23. Salutations from the *Akathistos Hymn*, Greek, fifth century, translated by Vincent McNabb, OP (Oxford: Blackfriars, 1947), n.p.

24. Saint Robert Southwell, SJ (1561–1595), *Collected Poems of St. Robert Southwell*, edited by Peter Davidson and Anne Sweeney (Manchester, UK: Carcanet Press Ltd., 2007).
    Author's note: Line 1: *Eva* (Latin for *Eve*) spelled backward is *Ave* (*Hail* in Latin), the first word of the angel's greeting to Mary. Many Catholic poets played on the words *Eva* or *Eve* (mother of humanity but cause of their fall) and *Ave* (*Hail* in Latin), the first word of the angel's greeting to Mary announcing that she was to bear Christ, the Savior of the world.

25. Saint Augustine of Hippo Regius (354–430), *On the Creed to the Candidates for Baptism*, 4, translated by Philip T. Weller (St. Louis, MO: B. Herder Book Co., 1959), 217–218.

26. Saint Ephrem of Edessa (ca. 306–373), *Hymns on the Church*, #37, translated by Sebastian Brock, in *The Luminous Eye* (Kalamazoo, MI: Cistercians Publications, 1992), 72–73.

27. James Quinn, SJ, *Praise for All Seasons* (Pittsburgh: Selah Publ., 1994), 106.

28. Blessed John Henry Newman (1801–1890), a devotional reading on St. Joseph in *Meditations and Devotions by John Henry Newman* (London: Longmans, Green and Co., 1893), 365–367.

29. Saint Robert Southwell, SJ (1561–1595), *The Complete Poems of Robert Southwell*, edited by Alexander B. Grosart (London, 1872; Greenwood Press, 1970), 126.

30. Saint John Chrysostom (ca. 347–407), *Metaphrastes,* July 2, *Roman Breviary in English* (New York: Benziger Brothers, Inc., 1951), summer volume, 633.
31. Epiphanius of Salamis (ca. 315–403), see F. C. Conybeare, "The Gospel Commentary of Epiphanius" on Luke, in *Zeitschrift fur die neutestamentliche Wissenschaft* 7 (1906), 318–332.
32. Hymn, © Stanbrook Abbey.
33. Saint Ambrose of Milan (ca. 340–397), Book 2 of his Commentary on St. Luke, chapter 2, near the end, from the *Roman Breviary,* John, Marquess of Bute (London and Edinburgh: William Blackwood and Sons, 1908), 902, alt.
34. Dag Hammarskjöld (1905–1961), in *Markings,* Leif Sjoberg and W. H. Auden (New York: Alfred A. Knopf, 1971), 195.
35. The Roman Proclamation of Christ's Birth, adapted from the old Roman Martyrology.
36. John Milton (1608–1674).
37. Saint Ephrem the Deacon (ca. 306–373), Nativity 16:11, translated by Sebastian Brock, in *The Luminous Eye* (Kalamazoo, MI: Cistercian Publications, 1992), 89.
38. Saint Robert Southwell, SJ (1561–1595), *The Complete Poems of Robert Southwell,* Alexander B. Grosart (London: 1872; Greenwood Press, 1970).
39. Saint Leo the Great († 461), PL 54, 190, in *A Short Breviary,* Fourth Edition (Collegeville, MN: Liturgical Press, 1949), 295.
40. St. John Chrysostom (ca. 347–407), *The Liturgy of Saint John Chrysostom,* translated by Joseph Raya and Jose de Vinck (Alleluia Press, 1970), 33.
41. Hymn, © 1985, the Community of Saint Mary the Virgin, Wantage, Oxfordshire.
42. St. Augustine of Hippo Regius (354–430). *Sermons for Christmas and Epiphany,* translated by Thomas C. Lawler (New York: Newman Press, 1952), Sermon 12, 2, pp. 122–123.

43. Saint Augustine of Hippo Regius (354–430). *Sermons for Christmas and Epiphany,* translated by Thomas C. Lawler (New York: Newman Press, 1952), 181.
44. *The New English Hymnal,* abbreviated and altered text, © 1986, The Canterbury Press, Norwich, NR3 3BH.
45. Saint Fulgentius of Ruspee, Tunisia (468–533), from *A Short Breviary,* Fourth Edition (Collegeville, MN: Liturgical Press, 1949), 302–303.
46. Saint Augustine of Hippo Regius (354–430), a fifteenth-century Christmas homily, in *Sermons for Christmas and Epiphany,* translated by Thomas C. Lawler (New York: Newman Press, 1952), 141.
47. Ralph Wright, OSB, © 1989, GIA Publications Inc., 7404 South Mason Ave., Chicago, IL: 60638.
48. St. Jerome of Bethlehem (ca. 342–420), from his Commentary on Paul's Epistle to the Galatians, III, 6, in the *Roman Breviary in English* (New York: Benziger Brothers, Inc., 1950), I, 355, alt.
49. Stanley Hauerwas, *Matthew* (Grand Rapids, MI: Brazos Press, 2006), 41.
50. St. Augustine of Hippo Regius (354–430), *Sermons for Christmas and Epiphany,* translated by Thomas C. Lawler (New York: Newman Press, 1952), Sermon 18, 2, p. 156.
51. Caelius Sedulius, *Hostis Herodis impie,* early fifth century, translated by Alan Gaunt, #90, 1–2, 5.
52. Saint Birgitta of Sweden (ca. 1303–1373), *Life and Selected Revelations,* translated by Albert Ryle Kezel (New York: Paulist Press, 1990), 131.
53. Saint Robert Southwell, SJ (1561–1595), *The Complete Poems of Robert Southwell,* edited by Alexander B. Grosart (London 1872; Greenwood Press, 1970), 134.
54. A hymn, altered from *Rex gloriose martyrum* (sixth century), © 1971, John Webster Grant.
55. T. S. Eliot (1888–1965), *Murder in the Cathedral,* 4th Edition (London: Faber and Faber, 1938), 74–75, 76.

56. The English translation of *The Roman Missal* © 2010, International Commission on English in the Liturgy Corporation.
57. Saint Robert Southwell, SJ (1561–1595), *The Complete Poems of Robert Southwell*, edited by Alexander B. Grosart (London 1872; Greenwood Press, 1970), 109.
58. Blessed Margaret Ebner, OP (1291–1351), *Major Works*, translated by Leonard P. Hindsley (New York: Paulist Press, 1993), 139.
59. The English translation of *The Roman Missal* © 2010, International Commission on English in the Liturgy Corporation.
60. To Our Blessed Lady. Henry Constable (1562–1613). http://www.sonnets.org/constable.htm#212.
61. St. John Chrysostom (ca. 347–407), from *The Short Breviary* (Collegeville, MN: The Liturgical Press, 1954), 694–695.
62. Te Deum, Part B, Copyright © 1988 English Language Liturgical Consultation.
63. Saint Hildegard of Bingen (1098–1179), translated by Barbara Newman in *Divine Inspiration: The Life of Jesus in World Poetry,* Robert Atwan, George Dardass, and Peggy Rosenthal, Eds. (New York: Oxford University Press, 1997), 9.
64. Charles Coffin, 1736; revised John Chandler, 1837.
65. Saint Bernard of Claivaux (1090–1153), Homily 1 on the Circumcision.
66. The English translation of *The Roman Missal* © 2010, International Commission on English in the Liturgy Corporation.
67. Blessed Margaret Ebner, OP (1291–1351), *Major Works*, translated by Leonard P. Hindsley (New York: Paulist Press, 1993), 140.
68. Saint Robert Southwell, SJ (1561–1595), *The Complete Poems of Robert Southwell,* edited by Alexander B. Grosart (London, UK: 1872; Greenwood Press, 1970).
69. Saint Augustine of Hippo Regius (354–430). *Sermons for Christmas and Epiphany,* translated by Thomas

C. Lawler (New York: Newman Press, 1952), Sermon 23, 1, p. 178.
70. Yves Congar, OP (1904–1995), *The Mystery of the Temple* (Westminster, MD: Newman Press, 1962).
71. Saint Robert Southwell, SJ (1561–1595), *The Complete Poems of Robert Southwell,* edited by Alexander B. Grosart (London, UK: 1872; Greenwood Press, 1970).
72. Saint Augustine of Hippo Regius (354–430). *Sermons for Christmas and Epiphany* (New York: Newman Press, 1952), Sermon 8, 4, p. 105.
73. Tridentine Liturgy, Feb. 2, translated by William G. Storey.
74. Saint Robert Southwell, SJ (1561–1595), *The Complete Poems of Robert Southwell,* edited by Alexander B. Grosart (London, UK: 1872; Greenwood Press, 1970), 135.

    Author's note: "Nazareth" signifies "a flower." The first two stanzas recount the return of the Holy Family to Nazareth and of Herod's dangerous son; the third stanza refers to the virginal incarnation and the crucifixion of Christ.

75. Stanley Hauerwas, *Matthew* (Grand Rapids, MI: Brazos Press, 2006), 42.
76. The English translation of *The Roman Missal* © 2010, International Commission on English in the Liturgy Corporation.
77. Saint Robert Southwell, SJ (1561–1595), *Collected Poems of St. Robert Southwell,* edited by Peter Davidson and Anne Sweeney (Manchester, UK: Carcanet Press Ltd., 2007).
78. Te Deum, Part B, Copyright © 1988 English Language Liturgical Consultation.
79. A Salutation to Our Lady, University College, MS, CLXXIX, Claire Kirchberger, Ed., *The Coasts of the Country* (Chicago: Henry Regnery, 1952), 27, alt.
80. Blessed Julian of Norwich (ca. 1342–1416), in *Revelation of Love*, chap. 4, translated by John Skinner (New York: Doubleday/Image Books,1997), 8–9.

81. Geoffrey Chaucer (ca. 1343–1400), "To Our Lady Mother," translated by Dolores Warwick Frese, professor of English, the University of Notre Dame. Used by permission.
82. R. S. Thomas (1913–2000), in *Divine Inspiration: The Life of Jesus in World Poetry,* Robert Atwan, George Dardass, and Peggy Rosenthal, Eds. (New York: Oxford University Press, 1997), 7.
83. Saint Ephrem of Edessa (ca. 306–373), *Hymns on the Church,* #37, translated by Sebastian Brock, in *The Luminous Eye* (Kalamazoo, MI: Cistercians Publications, 1992), 72–73.
84. Thomas of Celano, OFM (1185–1260), *The First Life of Saint Francis of Assisi,* Book I, Chapter 33, #84–86 in *The English Omnibus of the Sources for the Life of St. Francis,* 4th revised edition, Marion A. Habig, OFM, Ed. (Chicago, IL: Franciscan Herald Press, 1972), 300–301.
85. Blessed Pope John XXIII (1881–1963), a prayer during the Mass of New Year's Day, 1961, for the *Pueri Cantores* (Boy Singers) of many nations, in *Discorsi mesaggi, colloqui,* vol. III, 119.
86. Christina Rossetti (1830–1894), "A Christmas Carol."
87. Andrzej Morsztyn (ca. 1613–1693), in *Divine Inspiration: The Life of Jesus in World Poetry,* Robert Atwan, George Dardass, and Peggy Rosenthal, Eds. (New York: Oxford University Press, 1997), 15.
88. John Milton (1608–1674), "The Nativity of Christ."
89. Blessed Guerric of Igny († 1157), *The Christmas Sermons of Blessed Guerric of Igny,* Sermon 1, translated by Sister Rose of Lima (The Abbey of Gethsemani, 1959), 28.
90. *In Excelsis Gloria,* in *The Oxford Book of Carols,* Percy Dearmer, R. Vaughan Williams, and Martin Shaw (London: Oxford University Press, 1928/1964), #178.
91. A private devotion issued from the piety of the Capuchin Franciscan order.

92. Thomas Merton (1915–1968), *Carol* (Santa Barbara, CA: Unicorn Press, 1967).
93. Dante Alighieri (1265–1321), *The Divine Comedy*, Volume III, *Paradise*, Canto XXXIII, translated by Mark Musa (New York: Viking Penguin, 1986), lines 1–21.
94. *Tota pulchra es, Maria,* from the Tridentine Liturgy.
95. Saint Hildegard of Bingen (1098–1179), translated by Barbara Newman in *Divine Inspiration: The Life of Jesus in World Poetry,* Robert Atwan, George Dardass, and Peggy Rosenthal, Eds. (New York: Oxford University Press, 1997), 9.
96. Saint Robert Southwell, SJ (1561–1595), *The Complete Poems of Robert Southwell,* Alexander B. Grosart (London: 1872; Greenwood Press, 1970), 134.

Acknowledgments

Unless otherwise noted, all the Scripture quotations are taken from the New Revised Standard Version Bible: Catholic Edition, copyright © 1989, 1993 National Council of the Churches of Christ in the United States of America. Used by permission. All rights reserved.

Five excerpts taken from the *New American Bible revised edition* © 2010, 1991, 1986, 1970 Confraternity of Christian Doctrine, Washington, D.C. and are used by permission of the copyright owner. All Rights Reserved. No part of the *New American Bible* may be reproduced in any form without permission in writing from the copyright owner.

Three excerpts taken from *The Good News Bible: Today's English Version* (New York: The American Bible Society, 1992), TEV.

Eight psalms from *The Revised Grail Psalms* Copyright © 2010, Conception Abbey/The Grail, admin. by GIA Publications, Inc., www.giamusic.com. All rights reserved.

English translations of The Lord's Prayer, The Canticle of Zachary, The Canticle of the Virgin Mary, Te Deum Laudamus, part B © English Language Liturgical Consultation (ELLC), 1988, and used by permission. See www.englishtexts.org.

The English translation of the *Gloria in excelsis Deo* and the Greater Doxology from *The Roman Missal* © 2010, International Commission on English in the Liturgy Corporation. All rights reserved.

The Athanasian Creed from the *Roman Breviary in English*, Volume 1. New York: Benziger Brothers, Inc., 1950.

One hymn from Thomas Hopko, *The Winter Pascha*. Crestwood, NY: St. Vladimir's Seminary Press, 1997. Used by permission.

Two excerpts from Joseph Raya and Jose de Vinck in *Byzantine Daily Worship*. Allendale, NJ: Alleluia Press, 1969.

Four excerpts from *A Short Breviary*, Fourth Edition. Collegeville, MN: Liturgical Press, 1949.

Three hymns from the Stanbrook Abbey Hymnal © 1995, 1974, Wass, York.

Three excerpts from Robert Atwan, George Dardass, and Peggy Rosenthal, Editors, *Divine Inspiration: The Life of Jesus in World Poetry*. New York: Oxford University Press, 1997.

Two hymns of Saint Ephrem of Edessa, translated by Sebastian Brock, from *The Luminous Eye*.
Number CS124 in the Cistercian Studies Series, Copyright 1992 by Cistercian Publications.
A Cistercian Publications title published by Liturgical Press, Collegeville, MN.
Reprinted with permission.

"Joseph, We Praise You," from *Praise for All Seasons*. Text: © James Quinn, S.J., Selah Publishing Co., Inc., North American agent. www.selahpub.com.

A prayer of St. John Chrysostom, translated by Joseph Raya and Jose de Vinck from *The Liturgy of Saint John Chrysostom*. Allendale, NJ: Alleluia Press, 1970.

One hymn © 1985, the Community of St. Mary the Virgin, Wantage, Oxfordshire. Used by kind permission of the Community of St. Mary the Virgin.

Excerpt from T. S. Eliot, *Murder in the Cathedral,* 4th Edition. London: Faber and Faber, 1938.

"We Sing of That Disciple" by Ralph Wright, OSB. Copyright © 1989 by GIA Publications, Inc.
7404 S. Mason Ave., Chicago, IL 60638
www.giamusic.com. 800.442.1358
All rights reserved. Used by permission.

"To Our Lady Mother," Geoffrey Chaucer, translated by Dolores Warwick Frese, professor of English, University of Notre Dame. Used by permission.

One excerpt from Marion A. Habig, OFM, editor, *The English Omnibus of the Sources for the Life of St. Francis,* 4th revised edition. Chicago: Franciscan Herald Press, 1972.

Prayer of Pope John XXIII © 1961 Libreria Editrice Vaticana. Used by permission.

Excerpt from Dante Alighieri, Paradise, Canto XXXIII, *The Divine Comedy,* translated by Mark Musa. New York: Viking Penguin, 1986. Used by permission of Indiana University Press.

Every effort has been made to locate the copyright holders for the works used in this publication and to acknowledge the use of such works. Any mistakes or omissions will be corrected in the next printing of this book.

Prayers or other excerpts without attribution may be considered composed or translated by the author.

About the Author

William G. Storey is professor emeritus of Liturgy and Church History at the University of Notre Dame. He has compiled, translated, and edited many books of prayer, including *A Book of Marian Prayers, A Prayer Book of Catholic Devotions,* and *Novenas.* He currently resides in South Bend, Indiana.